ack Angus

Anderson is key speaker

Mississippi and the third largest nationwide.

Anderson credits a good part of his success in the restaurant industry to his ranching experience. He owns the 2,700-acre Black Angus/Cattle Company Ranch in Washington, where he raises and breeds Black Angus cattle. While neither Anderson's ranch or any single ranch has the capacity to supply the vast quantities of quality beef required by the chain, Anderson feels his ranching gives him an important edge in today's restaurant industry, by constantly keeping abreast of the ever-fluctuating beef and cattle markets.

Stuart Anderson

CITY HERALD, PASCO, KENNEWICK, RICHLAND, WASHINGTON

---

business

on rides high on Black Angus

gonna feel
inside."

erson's
ANGUS
NTS

Stuart Anderson raises the cattle used to stock restaurants under his name. (AP)

Black Angus magnate Stuart Anderson

---

dining and entertainment

Stuart Anderson

Profile of the man

behind the dream

by CARLA ANDERSON

In a city where the restaurant business is regarded as the most highly competitive, there is one name that comes to mind as newcomer of the pack. That name is Stuart Anderson.

As president of Black Angus Enterprises, Stuart Anderson now heads 45 restaurants for Saga Corporation, as well as serving as Saga's vice president of their restaurant division.

Hardly the story of a poor youth who struggled to success and fame. Stuart's story is rather one of an individual who succeeds at attaining all goals he has set.

And the goals have not been small ones.

This "quiet man who does not like being in the limelight," as he is described by Cartorian, has adopted "constant planning" as his watchword.

Stuart has worked all his life to build his empire, yet his empire is never completed. He simply moves ahead to new plans.

An active man who counts tennis and squash among his hobbies, Stuart is as at home on the sea as he is riding the range on his 2,600-acre Black Angus ranch.

His Groote Beer or Great Bear as the North star is often called, is a 50-foot sailing vessel, for boat seems too ordinary to describe this historical craft.

Stuart has owned the Groote Beer for six years and his face lights up as he talks about it.

"Did you ever hear of Hermann Goering?", he queries. He goes through a list of German names until he hits the more familiar name of Hitler. Upon seeing recognition of the name, he continues with his story

A Dutchman was commissioned by Goering, Hitler's Reichmarshal, to build the craft, which is embellished with carvings on the fine look inside and out as well as a fireplace.

"The builder did not want Goering to have it so purposely slowed up the making of the boat," he said.

The man got his wish, the boat never

Economy

Black Angus plans herd of new restaurants

by Boyd Burchard
Times business reporter

The Stuart Anderson Black Angus restaurant chain is poised to grow faster in the next five years than it did in the first 20, says its founding chairman.

"It took five years to open the first five (restaurants)," Stuart Anderson recalled at a recent celebration of the chain's 20th anniversary April 1.

"Now we're adding about one a month and expanding toward the East Coast."

The Eastern Washington cattleman opened the first Black Angus on Elliott Avenue in Seattle in 1964. The chain grew to 10 restaurants by 1972 when he sold the company to Saga Corp. of Menlo Park, Calif., in a multimillion dollar exchange of stock.

Today the chain, best known

Stuart Anderson
Served wrestlers and escargot

brimmed Stetson are recognized across the country.

The Stuart Anderson Bl Angus/Cattle Company alread the largest dinner-house chain v of the Mississippi and third-lar in the nation. The 8,000-emplo chain recently won the No ranking in a national-maga survey on customer satisfactio national restaurant chains.

Anderson lives at the 2,700-a Black Angus/Cattle Comp Ranch near Ellensburg, where raises and breeds Black An cattle. He credits a good part his restaurant-industry succes contact with the ever-fluctua beef and cattle markets.

Son of a country doctor, An son holds a degree in busir administration from the Univer of Washington.

While attending school in \

tlers and their followers.

In 1960, with the popularity of

Stuart Anderso

By Nicholas K. Geranios
Associated Press

THORP, Wash. — Black Angus restaurant chain founder Stuart Anderson is planning to sell his home on the range, and he says it's not because of any money problems.

"I am not in financial trouble," Anderson said, adding he was angered by the rumors that sprang up after the Oct. 4 auction of the ranch was announced.

He declined to reveal his net worth.

Disputes with the new owners of the chain are the main reason for the auction of the 2,500-acre Black Angus/Cattle Company Ranch located near Ellensburg, he said.

Stuart Anderson
Selling his home on the range

HERE'S THE BEEF!

STUART ANDERSON

PUBLISHING

Seattle, Washington

Published by
Hara Publishing
P.O. Box 19732
Seattle, WA 98109
(206) 775-7868

ISBN: 1-883697-94-8

Library of Congress Catalog Card Number: 96-079664

Manufactured in the United States
10 9 8 7 6 5 4 3 2

Sincere effort has been made to trace the ownership of all copyrighted picture material. If any question arises as to the use of any material, the author will be happy to make the necessary correction in future printings.

This book is not intended to replace professional medical advice. You should always consult your physician before changing your diet. The information in this book comes from sources believed to be reliable.

Supervising Editor: Vicki McCown
Cover Designer: Ron de Wilde
Format Designer: Shael Anderson

I dedicate this book
to the memory of
my mother and father

ACKNOWLEDGMENTS

I've always needed a lot of help with everything I've done in life and this book was no exception.

First and foremost, the best help I got was from my lover, my friend, and my roommate—my wife, Helen. Thanks!

I would also like to thank Sheryn of Hara Publishing for the push I needed, Mike and Vicki for correcting me, Kathleen for the indoctrination, Cyndy and Christopher for the readings, step-son Mike for the computer expertise, Ken Whitmire of Yakima, Washington, for his many photographs, and Patti, Lauren, Don, Paul, and Jay for technical data. A special thanks to my fellow bus drivers—the brain trust—Phil and Lisle for their ideas.

AUTHOR: *A fool who, not content with having bored those who have lived with him, insists on tormenting the generations to come.*
—Montesquieu

TABLE OF CONTENTS

BUYING BEEF
(AT THE SUPERMARKET)

COOKING BEEF
(IN THE KITCHEN)

• • • • • • • • • • • • • •

INTRODUCTION

I sat there on my tractor in the bean field watching the sun set in the Pacific when there came a moment in my life that remains frozen in my memory. Coming at me, right through the beans, was a huge, one-eyed monster making a horrendous racket and spitting fire and steam. It wasn't quite dark yet, but I could see the eye of this thing was bright with a hood over it like a bonnet. The whole field started to shake as it lumbered toward me. I hate to admit it, but I got more than somewhat spooked. I didn't expect anything like this in this quiet field. I probably looked like a deer caught in the headlights of a car. What had I gotten into?

I was just a kid on the first day of my new job. It was mid-season and I was trying to get some money for my freshman year at the University of Southern California. I had found work with the Janss Corporation out of Westwood, California. The temporary job was on the company ranch near Ventura, California, harvesting lima beans. It was my first experience farming and I loved it—but forget the lima beans! I've never put them on a menu nor do I eat them with any great glee. I knew the job was going to mean long hours, but no one prepared me for my fire-breathing apparition.

Right alongside the field where I worked was a railroad track that I hadn't noticed before. I suddenly became aware that my monster was a steam engine pulling the famous Daylight Train from San Francisco to L.A. The train had just left the city of Ventura and was chugging up a slight incline on its way to the Simi Valley and on to Los Angeles. It came within a couple of yards of me and about blew me off the tractor. It's hard to believe, but that magnificent engine was soon to become a thing of the past.

The hood on the headlight, I know now, was a seemingly useless precaution taken at the time of the blackout. It was 1942 and our country had just declared war so there was fear of invasion by the Japanese. The Ventura area became especially anxious following a surprise attack by a Japanese submarine off the coast of Goleta, near Santa Barbara, a short time before.

Because it wasn't quite dark, the window shades on the passing train had not been drawn, as required by blackout regulations. I stared with fascination into those windows, captivated by all the activities inside. The train appeared to be moving in slow motion. As the dining car and then the observation car clickity-clacked by, I had a revelation of sorts. The well-dressed passengers were living in the joy of the moment and they looked so glamorous and beautiful. This world of high excitement was made even more appealing by the envy of one lonely kid. As the cars disappeared, the red taillight bobbing as if waving good-bye, I was left wondering all kinds of thoughts.

It was at that moment I realized I couldn't get there, to the glamorous life of the people in those cars, from here, ranching for minimum wage. I knew then as I know now that ranching, as good as it is working with animals and being in the great outdoors, is hard work for low pay and wouldn't be a financially sound route to enjoying a ride on that train someday.

So—because of that experience, I don't think I was much of a rancher before I was a restaurateur. The purpose of this foreword is to explain the backward flow of my book. The logical path would be raising beef, buying it, cooking it, and selling it in restaurants. I've written this book in the order that I moved ahead in life, but you don't have to read it in that order. The four basic sections can be read in any order you find interesting—after all, it's your book. Do as you please.

Maybe you're asking yourself, "What is this book?" If you thought you were buying an autobiography, you've been had. Oh, there's some of that, but not enough to give it such a classification. Could it be a cookbook? Yes, but only insofar as some great treatments of beef and its partners are concerned. Maybe it's a business book? Sure, but not on a serious level. Is it self-serving? NO! I don't own any restaurants anymore, nor one head of cattle, nor one acre of ranch land. Is it pro-beef? You bet! Controversial? Yes. I hope you'll find the book interesting.

The restaurant came first, which is why I put the selling of beef out of the logical order of things. But before we leap ahead of ourselves, we must go back to the location of the train incident and my restaurant endeavors. In between, there came a dance with the devil—Adolf Hitler. He managed to alter our lives and take a few years out of my schedule.

Incidentally, Adolf was a vegetarian.

A technical note: Believe it or not, I got tired of seeing my name throughout the book. So, as you read, keep in mind that the following names are all interchangeable and are one and the same: Black Angus Restaurant(s), Cattle Company Restaurant(s), Stuart Anderson's Restaurant(s), all commonly referred to as stores.

My Monster

CHAPTER 1

THE BEST OF TIMES
THE WORST OF TIMES

What a glorious day! I had waited for this for a long time—a happy day—but I had a strong feeling something was wrong. This day we were opening the one hundredth Black Angus Restaurant in Ventura, California. Here I was, back where my dream had started. This was a goal long anticipated and planned for and everything was right with the world, except . . .

The opening crew was there and in place. The mayor of Ventura, John McWhorter, and I had been interviewed on TV and all the "suits" were down from the head office at Saga, the corporate daddy. The store (our label for restaurant) was completely finished for once. At almost all store openings between one and a hundred, work was still being done to complete the project.

It was our practice at a new location to have an experienced group of people from nearby Black Angus Restaurants, and some from the head office in Seattle, to be on duty for a day, a week, sometimes even for a month or more. The headquarters' staff attending opening night, including me and the vice presidents, would generally leave the very next day. It was also the practice, since so many of us were at the ribbon cutting, to have an informal business meeting the afternoon before the doors opened. This would usually be held in the room of whoever had the most space in the hotel where we were housed. On this particular day, no

Stu Who's News

Stuart Anderson's
BLACK / CATTLE
ANGUS / COMPANY
RESTAURANTS

Volume 10 Issue 4   February 1984

Black Angus Day Proclaimed in Ventura

Tim Klein, District Manager; Stuart Anderson; John Sweeney, Manager, receiving plaque at the 100th opening from Ventura Mayor John McWhorter.

Stuart Anderson's Black Angus/Cattle Company Restaurants Are #1

"For the third year in a row, **Restaurants & Institutions** has asked the American public to name its favorite restaurant chains.

And the 1983 winner is...**Stuart Anderson's Black Angus/Cattle Company**, which satisfied its customers better than any of the leading full-service restaurant chains. The Saga Corporation's chain of mid-priced steak restaurants beat out larger and better-known chains such as..." (continued on page 9)

Inside

Black Angus Restaurants' one hundreth restaurant opening

one remembered to tell me where the meeting location would be. I was busy with the media and didn't worry about it too much. I had noticed the top guys and gals weren't paying much attention to me. When I was free, I couldn't find anyone. Sometimes it takes me a little while, but I soon realized that I wasn't invited. Can you imagine what that did to my day? I was shocked and hurt but it did remind me of a recent decision I had made.

I'll give you a little background on why I shouldn't have been invited to any more operational meetings. About six months earlier, I'd talked with Jim Morrell from the president's office at Saga Corporation. (This is the company that now owned my restaurant chain, but you'll get the story on that transition later.) I expressed my feelings about all the meetings of the different Saga divisions, how they were a monumental waste of time, and how, considering my age, I felt it was appropriate for me to move on up to the honorary chairman. I would be directly involved with the public relations and marketing activities but not day-to-day operations, and certainly not the meetings. Jim, after talking to the other suits from Saga, accepted the change faster than I expected. Oh well, so much for feeling irreplaceable.

We then decided that the incoming president would come from the ranks of the big brother Saga Corporation—a large supplier of meals to business and college cafeterias and owner of a restaurant empire. This way we wouldn't disturb the working relationships among the existing five efficient vice presidents of the Black Angus chain.

I was somewhat involved with the selection of the incoming president, Ralph Pica, who was previously president of the Business and Industry Division of Saga, the contract feeders. I only knew Ralph through those frequent corporate meetings and felt we related well. He had no restaurant experience but seemed willing to learn; however, the vice presidents and other key employees kept coming to me for advice and decisions, and I didn't do much to discourage it.

When it came to the annual ranch meeting we held for all managers and headquarters' staff of the restaurant chain—some 150 participants—for fun, games, and business reports, guess who was the big wheel? Me, of course. Thinking back, I wouldn't want to have been in Ralph's position. So when I was eased out that day in Ventura, I should've been able to take it. Indeed, I asked for it. There may have been classier ways to bring it to my attention, but there it was. It was time to be reminded of my desires and get the hell out of the way.

The Ventura opening put a strain on the relationship between me as chairman and Ralph as president. The easy camaraderie wasn't there anymore. In retrospect, I'd felt I was prepared for the consequences in requesting the change of positions. Well, almost! I was prepared to find the ramp and get off the fast track, ready for a little less pay and bonus, ready for being in the office for only a short while. But there was one change I was not prepared for and that was the loss of power. From day one, since the first Black Angus, I was the boss and I hired and fired as I saw fit and didn't think much about it. As the business grew like a weed, I remained the boss and could do pretty much what I wanted—for better or worse. I don't think I ever realized what that power meant or what it carried with it. For some, power is everything—an aphrodisiac. I thought the dedication of my employees was given to me out of love, but perhaps it was the result of fear.

It was not that my fellow workers had to genuflect as I walked by. I was called "Stuart" or "Stu," and we did have a lot of fun. The atmosphere was always informal. Someone said that man's most awesome power is his ability to choose and I chose to leave that power behind without realizing how that would change things for me. I had my time. I had my fix. I just didn't realize how that loss of power would change relationships. Suddenly, people now opened the door for Ralph, hanging on his every word. I was opening my own door and being interrupted. I could see it all slipping away, but I decided to deal with it—it was over. My

ever-shrinking sphere of influence was something I learned to
live with, but it wasn't easy. I hadn't prepared for those changes
and I had to adjust to the human behavior of all those I had worked
with. That's life!

In the greater scheme of things, those moves were not to be
the last. In fact, Saga would disappear. In a few short years, a huge
corporation on the New York Stock Exchange would be no more.
The Black Angus chain was by far the largest contributor to the
profits of Saga. When Black Angus took a dip in that profit, the
suits put everything on the market—but that's another chapter. Hang
in there.

From one to one hundred stores was a long, tough, fun time
filled with interesting people, lots of luck, and some dumb decisions.
In hindsight, I would change some things, and in this book you'll
realize which ones. To those who say they wouldn't change a thing
in their life: Oh, come on!

Remembering that one hundredth store started the memories
and all the attending emotions. I began taking that long road back
to the beginning and gaining focus.

CHAPTER 2

IN A
NEW YORK MINUTE

I've always enjoyed reading biographies and autobiographies, but in most of the ones I've read, I have two long-standing objections. One is too much emphasis on childhood and early adolescence. They say the formative years are what shape a person. It may be true, but I generally skim or skip the early chapters and jump to the era that makes a particular person qualified to be the subject of a book. The second objection, and a real pain in the ass, is the sexual conquests by some sports figure or movie star. They're usually repetitious and by the dozen. I really can do without all that mattress surfing.

When I first started in business I lied about being older and grew a mustache to acquire a little respect. Later, when I lived on the ranch, I lied the other way around, but kept the mustache. We often gave hay rides around the upper part of the ranch to many groups of senior citizens, high-school graduates, business people, and so forth. I asked the fellows driving the people around how they liked the ride and what caught their interest. They all agreed there were three universal questions.

Question No. 3 was, *"How many cattle are on the ranch?"* (This is like asking you how much money you have in the bank.)

Question No. 2 was, *"How many acres make up the ranch?"*

The No. 1 question always was, *"How old is Stuart Anderson?"*

Senior citizens especially wanted to know my age. I don't understand why that should matter to people. I've lied so often even I get confused periodically, but I could always fall back on one interesting little fact. I was born on the very day of the exact year, month, and day the tomb of Egyptian King Tutankhamen was opened. The discovery is still considered the greatest archeological find of all time. After being enclosed for more than three millennia, the tomb was located and opened by archeologists Lord Carnarvon and Howard Carter, letting out all that 3300-year-old stale air on the very day I was born. When I first learned this, I asked my mother, "Do you suppose, since the opening was the exact time of my birth, that I might be . . . ?" When I saw the "like-I-gave-birth-to-this-child" expression on her face I dropped the subject and never brought it up again. Just as well that I leave it alone—there is that curse of King Tut, you know. Anyway, if anyone really wants to know my age, you can now look it up.

When I look back to my early years, I would like to make it full of drama and danger; but there wasn't any. My childhood was nearly perfect with a Norman Rockwell type of existence. At least for me, but I did give my folks some grief. I attended three high schools and my folks never moved. That's got to tell you something! I was the kind of kid my mother told me not to play with. We lived in Broadmoor, an exclusive conclave with a private golf course. In a way, I regret not suffering the pangs of the Depression. I don't mean to trivialize it to those who struggled through it; however, I did have to walk clear across the golf course to go back and forth to school each day.

My father never worked. He never cooked or did the dishes, he never mowed the lawn or washed the windows. Nor did he play golf or go fishing. He was a physician who practiced medicine day and night. He taught me that when you love what you do it's not work.

He became world famous in his field of orthopedic surgery. He was always looking for a better way, so he invented and held

Seated: my mother, Susan, and father, Dr. Roger Anderson. Laying down: our dog Tippy. Standing left to right, the three angels: me, sister Suzanne and brother Roger (Two out of three ain't bad.)

patents on orthopedic operating tables, leg splints and casts. He was at his peak earning ability during the Depression; consequently, instead of suffering as so many others were, we had maids to wait on us, and two Cadillacs in the garage.

I remember he used to ask my brother and me for the very latest jokes among our group of friends. He would use them in speeches he gave around the country. I attended a couple of these lectures, and when he came to the story we'd given him, I would hardly recognize it. I never could tell a good joke very well, much less remember it, but compared to him, I was hilarious. He knew what he was saying but his timing was terrible. I used to sink down in my chair with embarrassment when he tried to be funny. It was painful and I've never forgotten that feeling.

Both my brother and I were always known as Dr. Roger's sons while we were growing up and long afterward. I lived in the shadow of his fame. I remember people's comment: "Oh, that's Stuie, he's one of Dr. Roger's kids." My father couldn't have pleased me more than when, two months before he passed away, he told me he was proud to be known as Stuart Anderson's father.

I remember my father taking the train from St. Paul, Minnesota, to Fort Dodge, Iowa, to see his granddaughter a few days after her birth. Earlier that day, he had to be in St. Paul to bury his father. It was unlike his nature, but he was more than emotional as he said, "I've just seen one life leave this earth and now I get to see a new life come in." Twenty-some years later, my first-born spoke eloquently at my father's funeral which is always hard for anyone to do.

I miss him. He had a life that worked.

I know my daughters inherited good genes though. When the first one was born, she had seven great-grandparents—and I was twenty-six when I married, which was considered late in those days. When my second daughter was born about five years later, she had one great-grandparent.

After my stint in World War II with Patton's Third Army in Europe and then one more year at the University of Washington, I went to Fort Dodge. I was to help my grandfather, Dr. W. F. Carver, manage his office building, an eight-story structure with mostly professional offices. In the first three months, I more than doubled the rentals, which did not make me a lot of new friends! My grandfather was so good-hearted he wouldn't raise the rent despite the raging inflation at that time. Obviously, I didn't take after him. I had recently married Marilyn Smith in Boise, Idaho, and after the ceremony, we moved directly to Fort Dodge, so it was a honeymoon town where we found great friends. The tenants weren't crazy about me, but I was young enough not to give a damn. Also, my first daughter was born there, so I have fond memories of the place—and I learned a few lessons during that period.

Lesson No. 1: Don't anticipate the quirks of human nature.

The building had two elevators and three "boys" to keep them operating to all floors. I figured I could cut expenses tremendously by making the elevators automatic, which was a fairly new innovation and going strong in the big cities. Naturally the elevator operators had to go.

What actually happened was that when visitors pressed the button to open the doors, no attendant was there to greet them so they didn't get in. They stood there wondering what to do and finally decided to wait for the next elevator only to find the same empty space—no attendant. Some of the better-traveled people understood the new-fangled lifts, but too many of the country folks coming in to see their doctor or dentist turned around, found the stairs, and walked up to their floor. I wound up having to hire back an operator to man one of the elevators so everyone could conveniently get to the upper floors. Eventually, both elevators became fully automatic, but it took a couple of years and they didn't pay for themselves as quickly as I'd planned.

I will say this lesson helped me anticipate customers' reactions in later years as a restaurateur.

Four generations: my mother, daughter Christopher holding her son
Logan Gee, and me

My two daughters, Quincy and Christopher

Lesson No. 2: Watch your inventory!

Then came my next great move. There was some extra space in the lobby, so I installed a cigar stand with all the usual accompaniments. Smart move! It included a Coke machine which I decided to buy instead of lease. Later, when I took a pencil to that brilliant decision, I figured it would take me 21 years to pay for it.

Fool me once—shame on you; fool me twice—shame on me. I did it again. I bought chocolates for the holiday season by the ton at a great price and stored them behind the elevator shafts. What I didn't realize was that the elevators create heat. They melted all the chocolate. It smelled good for a while, but that was small consolation, and that sweet odor was a bitter reminder of my goof. Shame on me!

On my days off, I loved to drive out to the farms around Fort Dodge—the buckle on the corn belt. The farms were (and still are) well groomed and very productive, with numerous cattle in excellent shape. My grandparents were doing all right, thanks to the income generated by the increased rent, and I was inspired by the beautiful farms, so I decided to go back west and become a cowboy. I knew I wasn't going to make it selling chocolates!

W.F. Carver Building, Fort Dodge, Iowa

SECTION I

SELLING BEEF

(TO THE CUSTOMER)

CHAPTER 3

OUR ENDS ARE
IN OUR BEGINNINGS

I look to the future, but I can't help looking back.

I'm the type who likes to forget the wrong turns I've made in life, (along with the dumb decisions); however, the next move I made, as common as it is dumb, I always remember with a smile.

I had spent my time in the Army, had gotten some business experience under my belt, was married, and had my first-born child. After my Iowa adventures, I headed back to Seattle, wife and child in tow, to start a new chapter. I ended up moving in with "Mummy and Daddy" with all this baggage. They had a beautiful home on the shores of Lake Washington and I felt right at home. No rent, the food was good, and it wasn't costing anything. Made sense to me.

I began looking for work but it was summer and I wasn't in any big hurry. My baby daughter had just started to walk and she obviously felt compelled to run all over the house. She was one of those babies who could never sit still, and it was fun to watch her. Life was good. I had it made. Was this great or WHAT? Actually, it was an "or what." I smile now because I remember my father telling me that "no matter how large the house, it's never big enough for two mistresses." I was really pushing the envelope, and he never was one to let me get away with anything, so . . .

I went gently into that good night.

With my Army savings I bought a job and a place to live, all in one crazy move. I leased a small hotel in downtown Seattle with ninety ugly rooms, one of which was ours. It was the Caledonia Hotel at Seventh and Union. What a dump! It would make the Bates Motel look like the Waldorf-Astoria. (I'm not hurting the hotel's feelings because the old building died—it lies ten feet under the Seattle Freeway. There's nothing left but the memories.)

I worked the front desk and switchboard on the graveyard shift because I couldn't get anyone to work during the night in that neighborhood. Out of boredom I played a lot of pinball games in the lobby. Although few walking by would think of choosing my hotel, I did get some business from cab drops. If you're not familiar with the "drops," it worked this way: A cabby would pick up a passenger who'd ask the driver for a reasonable place to stay. He would take the fare to my "palace," then come back shortly to retrieve his dollar kickback for the favor. I paid out quite a few dollars every night. Sometimes the fare wouldn't like the room and I would be out all the way around. If I were lucky, the bellhop would tip me off that the guests were coming back down to the desk, and all of a sudden I would be very hard to find.

Included in the master lease was a small cafe that I subleased. Here was a real dump to go with the dumpy rooms. For months, the tenant wouldn't pay the rent so I reluctantly had to take over the operation, and that's how I got pushed into my lifetime career. I was the new operator of the Caledonia Grill. The bus station counter was its only competition.

Now, suddenly, I got lucky! The voters had recently approved the sale of liquor in the state of Washington and hotels were given preference for the licenses. As fast as I could I installed a small bar in the cavernous lobby of the dump. Hookers, seamen, hustlers, and wrestlers made up most of my trade. It was a very tough area and the opposite environment to which I was accustomed. I found

The Caledonia entry

it fascinating to work and mingle with my patrons who lived on the fringe. Most of them were always working angles or scheming something, except the hookers, who were there for their R&R. They worked out of houses in Alaska, and when the fishing season ended, they came to Seattle on vacation. They were great gals and I learned a lot from them—and we're not talking about sex either. You couldn't find a phony bone in their bodies. They were always up front, full of humor and loved to tease me. The people who sustained me in those crucial early years had few breaks in life but they made the best of them. I'm not ashamed of my humble business beginnings. Everyone has to start somewhere and it wasn't as if I'd sold my soul to the devil, but it was a life of seedy hotels, smoky bars, and blatant and blameless sex.

Since I couldn't name the bar "Hookers' Hangout," I called it "The Ringside Room" to entice the wrestlers and their followers from the Eagles' Auditorium across the street. Wrestling was just starting to be *show time*. I used a heavy hawser, which is a thick rope, instead of a normal bar rail. I recall one seaman who came in from an Alaskan tour. He loosened his belt, tied it around that huge rope, and announced he was there to do some heavy drinking. That's one way to tie one on. Then there was the day Mother, who was very much a lady, overcame her embarrassment at being seen in such an area to visit her "little boy." The bar was so small you had to squeeze by one of the stools to get to the other end. As my mother made this trek she brushed up against the stool's occupant, a wrestler, who grabbed back at his wallet and yelled, "Hey, watch it, sister!" That was her last visit to the dump.

In the early days, it was against state law to stand and drink and women couldn't sit at the bar. Federal law said we couldn't serve Indians. I ask you, can you always tell an Indian from a part-Indian from a non-Indian? It wasn't easy and I always gave them the benefit of the doubt for both our sakes. Sundays we couldn't serve liquor to anyone which meant we had to close Saturday night at midnight. That last rule meant shutting down a full house, and at times, I'd almost cry. In Washington State these were called the "Blue Laws" and they eventually changed.

I remember paying wages every week on Friday at six o'clock—the time the banks closed. I'm sure that created some hardships for many of those good people, but I needed the weekend business to cover those checks. To their requests to get their checks early, I told my employees, "No, no, no, sorry!" I couldn't tell them there was no money in the bank. None. They might get nervous and look for work elsewhere. Well, they know the truth now, and I hope they've forgiven me.

In fact, there were times cash was so tight I even tried banking out of town so I could gain time on mail transfers. Of course, that wouldn't work today with electronic banking, now, if the interest is in the bank's favor you can bet it'll be immediate, but if the interest is in your favor, it might take awhile.

I probably kept one of the lowest liquor inventories in town. Sometimes I'd have to send the bartender to the Washington State Liquor Store two doors up the street to purchase, at retail, a bottle of a slower-moving liquor because we just ran out of it. Then, as now, you had to buy your booze through state-run stores, using cash or certified check. Occasionally, the local liquor inspector would show up unannounced to see if your bottles had proper stamps on them. I didn't like the guy so I'd always try to get rid of him in a hurry, insisting I was too busy right then, or had some other important excuse. "Don't let the door hit you in the ass on your way out," I'd mumble under my breath. When I first met the inspector, he told me in a sly sort of way that he'd like to have enough money to buy a new hat every month. When I asked him why he needed so many hats, he just looked disgusted and walked away. He deserved to have that door hit him on the way out. He must've figured I was the dumbest bar operator on his beat. Maybe I was, but I never bought anyone a hat. In the early fifties in Seattle, kickbacks were an accepted practice. No one would even suggest such a thing now, I'm sure.

But here I am, winding down some old cow path and losing focus, so let me get back to where I was.

The Korean War was on and Seattle was booming. Being a port city, Seattle got a lot of servicemen. These were times when the hotel had more than a hundred percent occupancy—sometimes up to a hundred and fifteen. These were loose times and I felt like putting up a sign: "PLEASE REMEMBER THE NAME UNDER WHICH YOU REGISTERED."

The good news was the cash flow allowed me to make some improvements. I moved the hotel lobby to where the dumpy cafe was and put the dining room in the large hotel lobby space. I was a real restaurateur. I named it "The French Quarter" and I changed the lounge name to "The Downbeat Room," removing the famous rope rail in the process. As this was in the early fifties and stereo music was just coming of age, I placed two huge speakers at opposite ends of the lounge. I could simulate the sound of a train running right through the bar, or so it seemed on those great demonstration cassette tapes that came with the original stereo systems. It was a great gimmick, and the bar customers flocked to hear it.

Bill Teeter, an early associate, went with me to the Salvation Army to pick up old musical instruments—if they didn't play, all the better—and Bill placed them all over the back of the bar in an artistic design to go with our Downbeat theme. The new layout, emphasizing the stereo sound, along with a nice-looking dining area, brought in a different clientele, and eventually the hookers and wrestlers, uncomfortable with this traffic, moved on. I miss those teachers of life and wish them well wherever they might be. We also lost Bill Teeter (Del-Teet Furniture) as well as my buddy, Hughie, who's part of the story I'm about to tell. Both died far too early of cancer, leaving the world a little less bright.

I needed a bartender to go with the new setup. Hugh Klopfenstein (of family-owned Klopfenstein's, an up-scale clothing store), was an old friend and future roommate after my first divorce. He got around town a lot, so I asked him to find me a new bartender. That's how I came to hire Bruce Attebery, who eventually became my senior vice president. I checked him out at the tavern where he worked: young, barefoot, six-feet, nine-inches tall, and I realized he was singing along with the jukebox—my kind of guy! Everything fit except the feet. He'd have to find some size-fourteen shoes and put 'em on.

Bruce was a great bartender and continued his sing-along with Frank Sinatra and other old favorites on that wonderful stereo of ours. We did have one real conflict, though. One September, I started a promotion running a bus to the University of Washington football games with dinner and drinks. I asked Bruce to knock off the regular music on Saturdays and play all the football fight songs instead. All Saturday long, while the revelers were there, we listened to "Bow Down to Washington," "Fight, Fight, Fight, for Washington State," and other ditties. Bruce still wanted to whoop it up with Frankie. "Sorry," I told him, "but we've got to get into the old football spirit." And we did so, every Saturday when we had a home game.

When the last game of the season came, as the bus was getting ready to leave with everyone on board, I told Bruce he wouldn't have to play the records any longer. You'd think I'd untethered a monster. I heard the story later that he'd emptied the jukebox of all my beautiful records, took them out into the street, and used them for Frisbees, shouting obscenities as he threw each one. I didn't want to be there after the laughter stopped—some clean-up job!

Did this boy/man really become the senior vice president of the entire Stuart Anderson Restaurant chain? Sure, most everyone changes as they mature. He was very instrumental in the growth of the company.

We had everything going in the lounge except for a little sex appeal. I don't remember how, but I got hold of (not literally) two tall blondes—and I mean tall with legs up to their eye sockets—as servers. Now we had more than a little sex appeal. The two beautiful blondes were named, oddly enough, Sam and Jerri, and they became legends. Add micro-mini-skirts—the first in Seattle—to these big girls, combine them with the big bartender and the big speakers, and I was making it big!

I can't believe I forgot to tell you about the food. I tried a French menu with escargot and a lot of other French dishes I forgot the names of, but it didn't go over; the area and the building had been in the dumps for too long a time to do that menu any good. One Saturday night, I had nine people at the height of the dinner hour and five of them were family and I knew one of the other two couples. That tells you something. I have to learn things the hard way but I'm quick to adjust. It took me two months with the French menu before changing to a $1.95 steak dinner.

WHOA!

That's right—$1.95. The steaks were cut small and shipped in from Australia. They wouldn't quite grade "good" under our system today. This was a dramatic change but, except for the price, not an unusual menu for the time.

No pioneer me! I always considered a pioneer as a man with an ass full of arrows.

Now both lounge and dining room were starting to get some action. I had some more cash available, so along with a friend of mine, Fred McGuire, who had come into an inheritance, we bought a farm outside Redmond, a suburb of Seattle. Now my longed-for ranching experience was really beginning. The property had a small packing house on it. The meat I was getting off this property made the steaks coming out of Australia look like a piece of cardboard. The imported beef had to be tenderized, and if we didn't soak it enough, you'd swear you were eating leather. If the steaks were left in the liquid too long, it would fall off the fork before you could get it to your mouth. It was enough to turn you into a vegetarian. More on that later.

Anyway, I knew I had to move to all-choice steak from the good old U.S. of A. and raise the price accordingly. Even though the increase in price (to $2.95) was a leap of faith, it took me years to live down the serving of imported commercial steaks, which I did just short of a year. Even to this day there's a small number of people who still believe the restaurants serve tenderized or imported Australian beef. It takes a long time to live something down. The mistaken belief about our beef endured because our price was (and remains) well below the competition's, even after we started serving "choice."

To maintain that price, I had to turn those tables three times or more per night—in other words, serve three different groups at the same table during an evening. Not an easy feat. Also, we took no reservations—a move that created a constant waiting line. We had one-plate service and a limited dessert menu which helped shorten the turnover, along with no highchairs. Lose the kids— save the valuable table space. Mean!

I was looking to expand and take my format and gimmicks with me. The Seattle World's Fair had finished in 1962 and there was a lull in the economy. I found a closed and shuttered restaurant building and talked financing with an eager landlord. His name was Bayard McIntosh and he became a good friend. I told him I'd bring my formula but I needed some financing, and with my prices, I wouldn't be able to pay a percentage type of rent which was then the accepted practice. I'd like to think I took a page out of J. C. Penney, Wal*Mart, or Woolworth's Five and Dime—high volume and low margin, which leaves no room for a percent of gross. For example, my food costs hovered round fifty percent—far exceeding the norm. Using a one-plate service and highly competent people who could handle five or six tables at one time, I also managed to lighten the labor costs to help offset food costs. Rent, along with other occupancy expenditures, had to be kept low to make the formula function.

The location I was scouting was a famous Seattle restaurant called "Skipper's" and I remember being a customer when I was in high school. Since the war, it had fallen on hard times and changed hands twice. The last operators were Asians who called the place the "Double Joy" until they had to close the door. The building sat unused for months, and there's absolutely nothing worse than an empty restaurant that hasn't really been scrubbed clean. Ugly rats, putrid smells, and bugs of all kinds—you hear the scurrying of tiny feet the moment you open the door and turn on the lights. If my future customers had seen that sight, I don't believe they'd have ever come in those doors.

Before I could start a major clean-up and remodel of the building, I had to obtain a liquor license. Some dweeb on the liquor board (it's just as well I don't remember his name) said he couldn't grant me a license because of his crazy notion that if Asians and their family members couldn't make it, I certainly couldn't. I got an attorney and the landlord and we went to the state capitol in Olympia to plead our case to the entire Liquor Control Board. This one member was mouthing oxymorons about Asians in the restaurant business that had nothing to do with anything. We made our case, which was a good one, and got our license.

On April Fool's Day, 1964, we turned on the sign, opened the door, and got out of the way. The first Black Angus was open. They loved our selection of six different cuts of choice steak all at the same price of $2.95, which included a full dinner. People had never seen this kind of price, and it created such a waiting line that we had to tell diners it would be an hour or more before they could be served. That never stopped them from coming, and that line stayed with us, giving us a tremendous advantage in turning the tables, even as we expanded into other cities.

This sort of setup proved interesting in an unexpected way. That waiting line created a real source of games, tricks, stories, and human reactions of all kinds. I hope you don't recognize yourself in what's coming—but most of us will.

Some people felt that if they went into the lounge, they wouldn't be seated as quickly. Not true! Some felt if they sat close to the name-taker and stared at him or her, they'd get in faster. Not

The first Black Angus—1964

true! Then there were those who felt that if they got up and asked every five minutes where they were on the list, they'd get in sooner. Not true! None of the above. We honored that list at all times—no matter who you were. One exception—me! Well, maybe the President of The United States.

One night when a male customer was told it'd be an hour wait, he looked very indignant at the hostess and said, "Do you know who I am?" She quietly said, "No sir." He proudly proclaimed, "I'm Stuart Anderson!" She quickly replied, "It will still be an hour wait, sir." The hostess was my daughter, Quincy.

Over the years of working with a waiting line, you learn a great deal about people, even become an expert on human behavior. You start to think you know the status of everyone. There's a couple sitting in the bar who look straight ahead, rarely speaking, and if they do, they don't even look at each other. They appear rather unhappy, especially the man for some reason, and they want to be called to dinner NOW and get it over with. Couple Number One consists of two spouses married to the wrong person too long.

Then there's Couple Number Two. They can't get enough of each other. They don't look at anybody or anything—just each other. They don't care when they're called. You can see they have an expression that says, "Is it going to happen tonight?" You would love to move them down the list and move Couple Number One up. No way—the list is inviolable.

Couple Number Three looks nervous. Perhaps they're on a blind date. They won't recognize their name when it's called. You have to call it two or three times. Some people take the time to memorize two or three names above their own on the waiting list and when those names are called theirs had better be next. There are those who insist on looking at the list even though it's upside down to them. Just a word to those who might be anxious about it. Don't be discouraged by the "list" nor turned off by the amount of time the host is quoting you. Most people in charge estimate a time that is longer than actually expected. This way they alleviate some of the pressure on them and complaints about the wait. Not that it matters much anymore, since reservations generally are taken now that the marketplace has become more competitive.

When we opened Tacoma (the second Black Angus), we had the usual crush of business opening week. The store manager, Bruce Attebery, whom you've met, had his first experience in working with a waiting list and came upon what seemed like a great solution at first glance. Often guests arrived as couples rather than as four-somes and we didn't have enough two-tops (tables for two) but lots of four-tops (tables for four). Bruce went down the line asking each twosome if they'd like to meet their neighbor and make it a foursome. What are they going to say to the couple behind them while the six-foot, nine-inch boss stared at them? He managed to fill all those four-tops, and because the volume of business meant more in the cash register, I thought it was a great idea. On the drive home I started to wise up. Those people wouldn't be coming back despite the value.

To all the people from Tacoma who said, "You folks will never make it in that spot!" I have this to say: "Good call!" That particular store is no longer in operation. It had no parking and was in a poor location.

And you all ask again: This Bruce Attebery—he became your senior vice president?" "Yes," I say, "and a damn good one!"

One more story and I'll move along. My sister, who never tried to take advantage of her relationship to me in any of her visits to the restaurants, felt one time she needed to. After a ski weekend, she had to get back to a baby sitter so she told the maitre d' that she was my sister and couldn't wait the thirty minutes to be seated. The maitre d' said, "Yo, sure," then turned to a co-worker. "Hey Ed, we've got another one of Stuart's sisters here." Back to the end of the line. After hearing this story, I gave her my card saying, "This is my only sister." She had occasion to try it again. She gave the card to the name-taker who in turn gave it to the maitre d' who loudly proclaimed, "Hey, this lady is really enterprising and she should really get somewhere for her effort. How about back to the end of the line, sister!" I got this report later and was frankly pleased. I don't really want her to know how pleased I was to see the wait being honored, but it was and still is an important image to maintain. (I guess she knows now, but that's okay. One time, while talking on the phone, my brother and I were both wondering how we got to be first in line when they gave out sisters. How did we earn that?)

There came a time in the early development of this chain when some of my practices had a slightly sinister side to them. In the picture on the right, you'll notice what appears to be a vulture sitting on the shelf above my head. That's exactly what it represents and it was given to me by my cohort in picking up dead and dying restaurants—my attorney and friend in the early days, Dick Dameyer. These business practices had a dark side but, conversely, a glimmer of hope for someone's dying dream. This was the way it worked:

I was in contact with and romancing the credit manager of a large restaurant supply house. When this company had to take a truck over to some restaurant to pick up the stoves or tables and chairs because of a default on payments, I was there, swooping in like that vulture. The operator was about to see his (or her) dreams go down the toilet. I offered this person the opportunity to salvage some dignity and come out with something—that is, if I could make it go. Was I picking his bones or picking him up with a chance to start over somewhere else?

A dead or dying restaurant is a sad thing to see. Advertising stops when it's needed most as does the much-needed remodeling. The deliveries start coming C.O.D. and employees are nervous, depressed, and looking for other jobs. It's a vicious circle. This was the time I stepped in and started talking to all the parties involved, providing more hope than despair. I took over the lease so the restaurant operator didn't have to let the equipment be removed or file for bankruptcy and the employees could keep their jobs.

The vulture looking down on Helen and me—1974

Let's not forget the landlord through all this. He got excited about having a renter with a good reputation, even though he had to contribute some financing to help me remodel. Finding these situations and diving down to take advantage of the injured, was I a Prince of Darkness in a black hat or a savior? It's your call.

Before I made these vulture-style negotiations, I did my "sophisticated" (or should I say simple?) marketing research from whatever sources I had available: opening customer counts (number of customers per day counted by our sale receipts), interviews with start-up employees, customer and ex-customer opinions, and food and bar sale percentages. It was important to me to know if the previous owners had done a good business at one time. If their restaurant had enjoyed a brisk business in the first month or two, then their failure would more than likely have resulted from poor management. This could be caused by the wrong pricing, lousy service, kitchen stagnation, and/or all those operational faults that contribute to bad management.

As the chain grew, Ron Stephenson, vice president of development, worked with sophisticated site evaluations, and with great negotiating skills, he located many of the successful restaurant sites still operating today. Periodically, the two of us chartered private airplanes to go to different sites and study the general area, including traffic flow and population densities. We usually took a fun group from the office along for support. For a while Ron even used a service that gave us data on income, race, age, occupation, etc., within a one- to five-mile radius of the contemplated site. With all this research, Ron still used a lot of gut feeling before making the final decision and asked for the same from me, along with my blessing, of course. This kind of marketing research was also applied to "build-to-suit" operations which were in our future. The property owner would lease us the land, and either we or the landlord would build the restaurant to our specifications.

It took me eight years—from 1964 to 1972—to go from one to twelve Black Angus Restaurants. Financing was difficult and very complicated. Most of it came from two sources. First and foremost was the landlord who would often contribute building improvements and delay the rental payments. No one is more eager to do business than smart owners of empty buildings. They couldn't have been more cooperative. There was one rule I always observed in taking over a failing or a closed restaurant. I would change the appearance—exterior and interior—as much as possible, and with the landlord's participation. The time to deal with him or her is before you pay any rent or invest a dime. Once you get your operation rolling, the landlord is apt to become unavailable. I appreciated their involvement and I couldn't have done it without them. The second source was the food suppliers who extended long-term credit when I needed it the most. Some really compassionate people can be found in that business. I made sure they were paid on the committed date even if I had to put a second contract on my furniture (which you could do in those days).

There's an old adage in the hotel business: "If a room isn't sold for that night, its value is gone forever." This can apply to a table in a restaurant: "The most expensive item in a restaurant is an empty chair." Should a person go into this fascinating business when they may have to stare at empty seats and hate doing it? Should you? Answer these questions: (1) Are you willing to work long hours? (2) Do you enjoy being around lots of people? (3) Are you open-minded and tolerant? (4) Can you let go of your dream if it isn't working? and (5) Do you realize that to profit you must learn to please?

Plan to do something differently, and if different doesn't work, plan something else. In this business, there's no time for the hard work necessary to build it up. You'll run out of money unless you have a ton of it. I attended a seminar once where the so-called expert insisted that hard work—and more hard work—was the answer. Nonsense. Long hours, yes, but it better be fun. It's contagious and it's like a pebble in a pond—the ripple effect spreads throughout the whole room. Hire carefully and delegate with confidence. It's really very simple, but there's more on this in the next chapter.

Of course, I can't forget the banks and their involvement in the financing of these early stores. I had some notes with them but every one of those notes was co-signed by just about everybody—landlords or anyone who was handy. Do I sound like I'm critical of bankers? Not really. If I were a banker I would be nervous when a restaurant man came in looking for a loan. Eating establishments have about an eighty-five percent failure rate and bankers must consider that. What would you do?

The Bank doesn't serve steaks and we don't cash checks.

That's the saying we used to hang over our registers. Times have changed, of course. I think we both now violate these rules to some extent.

When we opened our third Black Angus in Spokane, Washington, we made every effort to divorce our operation from the accursed and competitive sister city of Seattle. We banked locally and used every scheme we could think of to disguise the fact our money went to Seattle. It was an exercise in futility. The Spokane customer—or customers from anywhere, for that matter—couldn't care less where you come from. Give any customer value and they won't care if you come from Iran during the hostage taking. Well, that might be a little extreme, but you get the message.

There was one last economical move I'll discuss that I didn't particularly enjoy. In fact, I wasn't very good at it. I had to take care of the bar before the lunch shift when a real bartender came aboard. It was only a couple of hours in the morning, but I've always been morning-impaired. I recall one incident that made that abundantly clear. Jim Greco was an architect from the firm of Bystrom and Greco who did a great deal of work for me on the early restaurants. (Arnie Bystrom eventually did my seafood venture, Stuart's at Shilshole, and is still going strong with good reason.)

Jim Greco came into the bar just before lunch, and after I greeted and served him, he muttered something under his breath. It was kind of like an "Oh, damn," but I wasn't ready for that, so I got really busy to avoid talking to him. He was clear down at the other end, but I could still hear him grousing about something. It's a known fact that bartenders are obliged to listen to a patron's trials and tribulations, but not me if I can help it. Here was Jim groaning again, and he was a good friend and customer, and important to my design work, so I felt guilty enough to at least hear him out. I dragged myself down to his end of the bar, took a deep breath and got the strength to ask, "Okay, okay, it kinda sounds like you've got a problem, so let's hear it! What is it? I'm listening."

"Well, I'll tell you what, Stuart—it's none of your damn business!"

That's just one of a thousand such stories in this crazy business.

OUR ENDS ARE
IN OUR BEGINNINGS

CHAPTER 4

THE CURTAIN
RISES

The restaurant business fit me to a tee. It would let me sleep late. Not that it was short hours; it was anything but—especially in the early years. It's a career that carries with it some of the longest hours of any profession a person can choose. Normal hours in the restaurant for me were from ten a.m. to eight or nine p.m., six days a week.

One day, my body got confused with the ranch life where I got up with the sun many mornings, and I ended up at the restaurant early with nothing to do. People didn't expect to see me and I had time to experience something rather spellbinding.

My first office overlooked the parking lot of the Number One Black Angus and faced toward the service door. I noticed a lot of delivery trucks moving around—I expected to see them—but the other people I saw going through that door threw me. They arrived in scruffy clothes, one at a time, appearing as though they had not been home for a while. Some wore bandannas; others resembled flashers with their bare legs sticking out from under their coats. They would knock and be admitted, this sorry-looking bunch. I didn't know who they were. But I figured they had to be my beautiful employees.

I don't think customers coming to our restaurants realize how much is involved or what goes on beforehand. Everyone has spent some time in a restaurant for lunch or dinner, and I thank all of you. However, it's quite something else before that curtain rises. You'd be surprised at how different the atmosphere is from what you might expect.

Employees start arriving between seven and nine a.m. You need a password to get in, but I doubt you'd really care to enter. It's noisy in there! The radio's blasting rock'n'roll music, pots and pans are banging, someone's telling a dirty joke, dishes are clanging—you can hardly hear the heavy-duty, commercial vacuum cleaner over all the other racket. The harsh working lights are blazing so brightly, you'd swear you were in a furniture warehouse that was on fire. The bartender is counting his opening cash till. It's a totally different look than it is when the customers arrive. It's fascinating to listen to the jokes, fun put-downs and teasing, but you also know that everyone's watching the time.

This is show business—more so than most other businesses I know. Everyday it's a stage setting, a major production, second only to the quality of the food. As the opening hour approaches, all of a sudden the tempo increases. The employees whom I didn't recognize earlier, hit the lockers and reappear decked out in their uniforms.

This was the sixties, and I'll be honest with you, the uniforms our gals wore were provocative. I can't think of any one thing that gave us more grief than how these gals reacted, whether positively or negatively. At first we asked for feedback at our in-store meetings. BIG MISTAKE! It was like opening a floodgate. They couldn't agree among themselves. What looked good on one didn't on another. It became an off-limits subject at all subsequent meetings.

One of the young gals, Sally Johnson Newbury, who worked for me a long time and is still a friend, likes to tell a story on me and my uniforms. She says, "When I was interviewed for work at the French Quarter, Stuart held up what appeared to be two handkerchiefs and told me to go back to the dressing room and put them on. I about died, but I wanted the work, so I put the outfit on and returned to his office, and he immediately said 'Okay, you start at five o'clock.'" This is obviously an exaggeration, but these gals were attractive by my standards and they had a great deal to do with increased business. In the days of the early sixties I could say, "Hey, with that body you could go places!" and they would smile and say thank you. I wouldn't dare say that today! Sexist or not, those outfits did work their enchantment on me and many others.

Incidentally, I'm sure I've been "politically incorrect" a number of times so far in this book. I shouldn't call ladies "girls" or "gals," I shouldn't have hired only women to work the floor, I should call them "serving persons" instead of "waitresses," and I certainly shouldn't have insisted they wear sexually provocative costumes. But that was then and this is now. Sorry, ladies.

Speaking of personnel, I recall a meeting in San Francisco where a stock analyst was discussing equal opportunities for employees. He asked me, "Is your company broken down by sex?" I told him, "That's not our problem—alcohol maybe, but not sex." After some strange looks, I thought I'd better get back to business and told them the numbers they were looking for—approximately fifty-five to forty-five ratio, women employees being the higher number of the two.

Anyway, I was talking about show business. It's time to open the doors. Someone now turns off the harsh lights, puts on the mood lighting, shuts down the rock'n'roll, and replaces it with background music. They're ready. The manager says, "Let's go to work," so the curtain rises and the door is opened to you, the customers.

It may start slowly but during the next several hours, nearly five hundred people will come and go at a Stuart Anderson's. Everything escalates. The atmosphere comes alive. The hum of the voices blends with the music, smoke from steak platters drifts upward, tantalizing odors waft from passing trays—all these and more become part of the atmosphere. The employees now are all business. They're smiling at the customers, but the interplay between them is gone. Now they're helping each other make the public happy.

Conservative costumes for the early days

One of the good things about this business is that it creates loyalty and comaraderie among all those working on this stage. If any one person stops working for whatever reason, things will slowly grind to a halt. It doesn't matter if it's the dishwasher, cashier, hostess, bartender, cook, busser, or whoever. They must all work together and help each other. There's no other way. It's like having a built-in check-and-balance system. I only wish this worked as well on the ranch. If I sent one of the hands out to the North Forty to fix fence and he goofed off and took a little nap, it wouldn't directly affect the other hands. Think about it, no way could he bring a halt to the entire operation of the ranch. The point I'm trying to make is that, in the restaurant business, the employees have a strong need for each other. If the dishwasher quits doing his job, there'll be nothing to eat off of; if the buspersons stop, there'll be no clean tables at which to eat; if the servers quit, the food won't get to the tables hot and garnished, if at all. You get the picture.

I had many faithful and dedicated restaurant employees. Most of my key management personnel, as well as many of the restaurant employees, stayed with me until my retirement. Many are still with the company. It was one of the most important parts of my success—selecting the best person for the right job. It's sort of like a good conductor: he can't play each instrument individually but he knows how they should perform together. The ranch was a different story. I just couldn't get or keep decent help. If they were really good, I guess they successfully operated their own farm and didn't feel they had to work for someone else. In retrospect, I may have asked too much of them. It's hard to say.

After the lunch crowd, everything begins to slow, the short-term workers leave and the full-time help relaxes until the curtain rises again for the evening performance. Now there are two shows: one in the dining room and one in the lounge. If the customers leave happy, it means they liked the show. If you ask each one why, you'll probably hear about the food or the service. They don't always realize the overall part the atmosphere played in creating their satisfaction. Lots of times I would ask my dining partner, after we had left an eating establishment, to describe the carpet, ceiling, music, tablecloths, or what the servers were wearing. It's amazing how few of the things that make up our surroundings can be recalled. They are all very much a part of the aura of our space—whether home, office, or restaurant. What is this thing called atmosphere? It's nebulous and as hard to define as it is to create. However, if you don't try—or if you miss—you have to operate entirely on the quality of food and pricing. In this competitive business, that might not be enough. You need every edge you can get.

It's our duty and obligation as restaurateurs to fill this need for our customers' comfort and for our own profit. What a crying shame if we didn't live up to our obligation to dress up the production and create excitement with fantastic background and decor!

Some of that which made the Black Angus unique in the beginning evolved quite by accident. One day I went to Del Teet Furniture in Seattle to have lunch with my friend and sometime-investor, Bill Teeter, whom you met earlier. He owned the store and was a well-known decorator. While waiting, I glanced around the store and noticed he had separated his room displays with sheets of clear plastic. I asked him if he thought we could separate our booths and tables with this see-through (Plexiglas) material. Customers would still be able to see throughout the room but keep their privacy, and cigarette smoke would go up to the ventilators instead of into a neighbor's face. Bill thought it was a great idea, and this feature became a standard throughout the chain. It was always appreciated—especially by the power-lunch bunch and those involved in intimate affairs which are always a part of the restaurant business. In using these dividers we created a special space; it looked right and it felt right even though it had special cleaning problems caused by static electricity. It was unique!

Bill came through in other ways. He helped me experiment with different table heights, sizes, and coverings (plasticized wood tops with logo insets, table cloths, that sort of thing) and with the lighting at each table. We tried candles without much success. Dripping was a problem as well as fire and accident hazards, which insurance companies frown upon. It's a known fact that women prefer candlelight and men like to see what they're eating, so we compromised. We put a little more light on the table with a Scandinavian wooden fixture that hung not so low that it would hide your partner but not so high you had to stare at the bulb. Unknowingly, we had established another Black Angus signature.

Other than the actual ranch photos and real Washington State-registered brands, the Black Angus Restaurants never had paraphernalia such as horseshoes, ropes, stirrups, or a saddle in its stage setting. Nothing against those items, they just seemed too typical. We did use something from the ranch, though: real barnwood bleached from the sun, spattered with moss, with square nails sticking out and lots of knotholes. I had old falling-down barns and some of my neighbors didn't mind my cleaning up their junk barns, at least for a while. Pretty soon they realized there was value there and the free-loading was over. When my expansion began, we ran out of real barnwood, so we created old barnwood by using acid. Not bad, but not great either. In any event, it worked and I stopped my search of worldly treasures—my lovely old barnwood. I miss the hunt.

So many restaurants achieve early success with gimmicks. That's all very well and good, but for the long, successful run you need to perfect the quality of your food and the efficiency of your service first. Gimmicks by their very nature die out fast; they're nothing more than a starter on an engine.

THE MOST IMPORTANT PERSON

Another activity behind the scenes and before the curtain went up was the meeting with all the employees. Fun? Well, yes, for me anyway. Actually, I felt you could never learn anything worthwhile at a meeting—unless the leader or moderator shut up, listened, and limited the time.

The day before we opened a restaurant, a meeting was scheduled with all new employees. I always had a ball with the group, kidding and teasing, but forever hoping to make some serious points too. Approximately one hundred new people were included in opening a restaurant—mostly young, mostly nervous.

Without introducing myself, I'd start talking. "Who's the most important person in the restaurant?" I'd ask, pointing to a young guy or gal for an answer. The response was usually a nervous: "You are!"

"And who am I?"

"You're the owner, with his name everywhere out in front and on the walls."

"That might be, but you're wrong about the most important person! It's not me. Try again."

"My new manager?" someone yelled.

"Nope! Who is it?"

From somewhere the answer would finally come back: "THE CUSTOMER!" (I believe they got a whole lot of help from the trainers.)

"Right. They are the most important." I would give the person a compliment for helping out and tell him or her that I knew they'd do great in their work. At our meeting we'd emphasize the customer is important but not "always right." That old catch phrase is too broad. Important, yes. "Always right," not necessarily so. There are times you must back your employee. I'm sorry to say that some real jerks exist out there.

I would go on to tell them: "About three out of every four people you see here will make it, so tomorrow try really hard and you'll find it worth the effort. Look around you. Some of the people here will become your very good friends. Do remember, though, that employees are not allowed to date and still continue working at the same restaurant." (This is like trying to hold back the tide.) "Now, take a minute and say hello to the people around you."

I'd continue: "Now, I'd like to give this microphone to someone here to tell us about yourself." I'd move through the group. "Why is everyone looking the other way? Okay, if you felt a moment of fear, that's natural. My point is, it should be the last time you feel fear in this restaurant. We do not operate by fear—it's not the atmosphere we want or will allow.

"We will pay you for the hours you punch on the time clock, but we have to earn the extra effort you put into those hours. We have a saying for all you food servers and that is: 'The last three feet is where it happens.' The future of this restaurant depends on what happens in that space. Most important, be your natural self. We don't script our servers."

I end with, "You'll be encouraged to take part in the monthly meetings and be part of this family. There are some rules and no-no's and I'll let your manager run through those. And here he is . . . ." Always give the no-no's and boring things to someone else.

IN MY OFFICE NOW

Does it sound like I scram when the unpleasant side of the meeting starts? You're right! It's one of the perks of being the founder. However, when it came to the vice presidents and the directors, if any discipline was needed, it was by yours truly. This especially brings back the memory of one incident, which was a watershed moment of my great ability to discipline.

I always gave lots of rein to my key people, many of whom had to travel to various locations needing their particular attention or talent. That is a decision I usually let them make. However, the "leader of our bands," Bob Anderson (no relation, but a good friend), who was our entertainment director, was traveling too many times to one particular city. He was in charge of placing live groups or deejays in the restaurant lounges, and with close to a hundred locations spread over the western United States, this was a demanding position and a hefty amount in our budget. I remember one time when an IRS agent was reviewing our books, he noticed the entertainment account and exclaimed, "Oh my, this is big. You people really must have a good time." We changed the name of that account in a hurry!

Bob was traveling far too often to lovely San Diego and that immediately raised a warning flag. It appeared he was abusing his travel privileges for personal reasons and something had to be done. Because Bob reported directly to me, this serious violation was mine to handle. Bob was young, tall, blond, handsome, single, and had a great wit—a dangerous combination. Now, I'm not prone to giving anyone a bad time, so to get in the right mood I spent the morning recalling all the bad things that had ever happened to me such as divorces and the price of same, misadventures in the stock market—especially the commodities, the loan to a "friend" who never paid it back, and so forth. When I felt I was thinking mean enough, I called Bob and said, "Into my office, NOW!"

What I wasn't prepared for was his new hair-do. He had gone out and got a curly permanent which was the thing to do at that time. His head was full of tiny little curls, and when I saw this silly-looking head, I knew I was in trouble. He looked like he'd stuck his finger in a huge light socket. I started to lose it. I peered down at my desk as I strained to tell him I'd have to red flag his personnel record. My mouth tightened and it sounded like someone else talking. Looking up at Bob, all I could see were the kinky curls and I just couldn't keep my mean mood. I tried hard to maintain control and stop the desk from shaking. You know that feeling when somebody farts in church and you fight to keep from breaking up? It happens. I felt like a little kid because it was happening again. How are you going to be tough when you're almost out of control? I told him to go away and come back another day, but as he was leaving, I took one last glance at the back of his head and totally lost it. You can imagine what this did to my tough image! I guess I wasn't the only one who reacted this way because, a couple of days later, he had his hair straightened.

NOW, WITHOUT WARNING, TEST TIME

Periodically I would have a business meeting with the vice presidents, directors, and district and store managers. One of my nicer nicknames was "The Quiz Master" because of the written tests I gave at these meetings. Of course, I knew all the answers and I liked to look smart. In the first section I asked approximately fifty specific questions about their store or district, such as:

		% of gross
(1) What is your laundry cost?	$	%
(2) What is your bar labor cost?	$	%
(3) What is your current food cost?	$	%
(4) What is your highest selling lunch special?		

Et cetera.

Obviously, I don't expect the reader to answer the above questions, but you might like to try these. Remember, this is the restaurant business. (The answers are at the end of the chapter.)

(1) What do we consider the most important ability for a manager:

    (a) Communications upward
    (b) Communications downward
    (c) Sociability
    (d) Ability to delegate

(2) In seeking to create customer satisfaction, the most vital thing to remember is:

    (a) We must promptly adjust all customer complaints
    (b) We must know what the customer wants
    (c) Employees create the customer satisfaction
    (d) We must have a good chef

(3)   The best treatment for grapevine rumors is to:

    (a)   Ignore them
    (b)   Find out who starts them
    (c)   Combat them with the truth
    (d)   Fire the rumor-mongers

(4)   Discharge of employees is more often caused by lack of:

    (a)   Knowledge
    (b)   Ability
    (c)   Social understanding
    (d)   Skill

(5)   If a restaurant is losing volume and money, the first thing the manager should do is:

    (a)   Analyze costs
    (b)   Study employee performance
    (c)   Study his own performance
    (d)   Make a chart & graph and see his banker

(6)   The most basic thing to remember in employee discipline is:

    (a)   Don't put it off
    (b)   Allow a cooling-off period
    (c)   Get all the facts
    (d)   Make an example of the case

(7)   What are the approximate average sales per employee per year in our restaurants:

    (a) $250,000
    (b) $100,000
    (c) $ 25,000
    (d) $ 10,000

(8)   Would the above sales be considered high or low
      in the top 500 industries:

   (a)   High
   (b)   Average
   (c)   Low
   (d)   Who really cares?

In the third and last section I finished with my "killer quiz," and if they got the answers in advance, all the better. You'll see what I mean.

"All right, everybody, write down as many of your employees names as you can—first and last. Next, the spouses' names and, if you can, how many children they have. Good luck!"

There were no one hundred percent winners, but you must remember there were seventy to eighty employees, full- and part-time, in each restaurant. Those managers with the highest percentages always seemed to have the highest morale. If any one of them wanted to cheat—write the answers down on their cuff for next time—it served its purpose.

Before anyone wants to even consider the above multiple choices, I want to give a dissertation on the Stuart Anderson School of Restaurant Management.

Some textbooks, some of the suits at Saga and, maybe, some of the readers might take exception to where I place almost all of the emphasis in hiring, training, and motivating. You can't train charm, personality, or attitude. You'll find these assets in your in-depth interviewing. I have always sought those people who would join in and become a member of a family atmosphere. (More on this later in Chapter Seven.) Motivation is ongoing and accomplished by treating all employees with great respect and appreciation for the many things they do.

One thing to remember: Most of our new employees are young adults (eighteen to twenty-six) who are not looking for long-term, career opportunities but simply want to earn money for school or increase the family income in the early years of marriage. Labor turnover is a given in the restaurant business. However, the Stuart Anderson Chain has one of the lowest rates in the hospitality industry. Some do stay with us a long time and may the sun shine warmly on their faces.

Now, I know you can answer the above multiple-choice questions. Try them again.

All the correct answers are (c).

Incidentally, if you happened to have guessed (a) on Question No. 7, which is $250,000 per employee per year in sales, that is closer to the beef-packing business which is one of the highest. The $25,000 per year represented by the employees of the restaurant industry shows just how people-oriented this business is.

WHEN BAD THINGS HAPPEN
TO GOOD PEOPLE

The restaurant business has always been very much a cash business. Many businessmen out there envy us because of that, but there are disadvantages. Almost every employee on the floor handles cash, which allows theft to raise its ugly head. How much of it actually sticks to where it doesn't belong is less than most people think.

I'm not proud about what I'm going to tell you now, but years ago, we hired a surveillance service to spy on our people, who were informed this was our practice when we hired them. A report would come back like this: "My name is Bob Smith and I arrived at the Black Angus on Elliott Avenue at 11:25 a.m. on Thursday, May 8, 1972, and entered the bar. The bartender, who I later found out was called Ed, said good morning and what's my pleasure. He had a vest on but no tie and his fly was half open. I had a bourbon and water and gave him a five dollar bill. He rang the till and gave me three ones and two quarters. He didn't talk to me but spent his time at the service window talking to the waitresses. I observed him drinking his mistakes. At 11:46 another bar man came in, who I later found out was Tom. He had on a vest and tie and told Ed to zip up. Ed did and put on a tie."

This might continue on and on for four pages. What did it tell us? Not much. Basically that this practice was a waste of a man's time and our liquor. It gave me a feeling of Big Brother when I read the reports. I quit the practice after a few reports didn't show much, chalking it up as an expensive lesson.

The best control I found was to interview and hire with great care and then treat all the people with respect. The vast majority of restaurant employees are honest and don't want to work in an atmosphere where light fingers are operating. They usually report them. In essence, your people become your theft control. Pretty nifty, huh? It's better to be taken a few times than distrust everyone all the time. Putting it another way, it's better to be occasionally cheated than perpetually suspicious.

Theft from the outside, however, became more of a problem. We worked with this increasing crime by using bigger and better safes, installing heavier doors with peepholes, and training the employees. Even so, there are always moments of exposure—the time safes are opened, when deposits are made, and of course there's the trip to the bank.

There was one case where our attempted solution to the problem bit us in the butt. My bookkeeper was nervous about taking the receipts from the restaurant to the bank, so I delegated this job to a "gofer," a big guy who worked for us for more than a year. This guy took the deposits by a different route every time. One day the route took this overweight fart away forever. It was a big weekend deposit and we were self-insured, which meant there wasn't an insurance company to collect from. Even after twenty-five years I find myself looking for him, but that train has already left the station.

One time we got burned even worse. Following another big weekend at our Spokane store, the first employee to arrive that Monday morning—an assistant cook—was confronted by three gunmen in the kitchen. They asked him to open the safe, which of course he didn't know how to do. The gunmen then put him in the large, refrigerated walk-in, and as others arrived, they, too, were escorted to the walk-in, which was kept at thirty-eight degrees. It was summertime—short-sleeved shirt weather—so you can imagine how these eight or nine early arrivals suffered.

About 9:30 a.m., our bookkeeper arrived. She emphatically told the gunmen she didn't have the combination, so into the walk-in she went to face the others, frozen in their light clothing, who knew damn well she had the numbers for the safe. They quickly convinced her this was no walk on the beach. Reluctantly, she knocked and told the bandits she would open the safe. I appreciated her earlier attempt, but the company's instruction has always been never to take risks—give them what they want. The three gunmen were apprehended but served no time on some technicality. That subject warrants a whole other book.

We are left armed with nothing but our tears.

CHAPTER 5

THE DAYS OF
WINE AND ROSES

When I got to the point of opening twelve Black Angus Restaurants and was operating each as a separate corporation, I was swamped with paperwork. The purpose of having that many corporations was to prevent one or two bad operations from dragging down the successful ones. Actually, all twelve were profitable and had positive cash flows, which I kept using for expansion. Even so, I was getting tired of the corporate meetings, and financially I was personally still hanging way out there in no-man's land.

The search for help from a "big daddy" had some options. Forget the banks—they got nervous every time they saw me coming. There was a remote chance to go public with a stock issue, but I didn't have a long enough history of earnings. You know the old saying: "When you don't need the money, it's easy to get."

About this time, I started pursuing a third option which was to find a large company with cash reserves and arrange a compatible marriage. I traveled around the country with a merger specialist and found a possible company in the Midwest and one in the deep South. In one I didn't like the personalities involved—we didn't seem to mesh—and in the other one I didn't like the grim offices, nor the people who looked just as grim. Eventually, in my quest for the "Golden Grail," I ran into Saga Corporation which was comprised of college, university, and business and industry contracted feeding. They also had limited restaurant experience with the Straw Hat Pizza places and Velvet Turtle dinner houses.

I got to know the Velvet Turtle restaurants before I ran across Saga. In my travels, while researching new locations for Black Angus, I became attached to one particular Velvet Turtle in the California market. They featured display cooking (beef, of course) in the lobby as you entered the building. The exterior and interior were tastefully done. At the time, I had no idea that we would become half-assed partners in the search for growth.

Wally Botello, the founder of Velvet Turtles, was to become a good friend. I learned much at the feet of the "master," as I used to call him. Wally had panache in whatever he did. I stayed with him at his Palm Springs townhouse and was totally impressed by his interior design. My raves about his decor would eventually lead to a major gamble on my part.

Wally introduced me to the world-renowned interior designer Steven Chase of Palm Springs, Singapore, New York, and other exotic places. (At that time he was with Arthur Elrod and Associates.) Steve had done Wally's home and I decided I wanted him to do something for me. Steve became involved with me in my grand experiment in seafood. (That's right, seafood—but more on that later.)

I'm saddened to say Steve is gone now. So is Wally after building his five-store chain to twenty-one restaurants with Saga. Incidentally, twenty of the twenty-one Velvet Turtles are also long gone, but before Wally left us, he built and operated Wally's Desert Turtle in Palm Desert, California. This is one of the renowned restaurants in the country and ably operated by his children. The story of Wally's departure from Saga is a mystery to most of us who knew and worked with him. A new Velvet Turtle was opening in Texas and a big banquet had been booked. The restaurant got paid for it, were informed no one would be attending and the liquor people didn't want a refund. So began the mystery. Why would someone pay big bucks for a banquet and not use it?

Wally Botello

Operating like Washington, D.C., lobbyists, liquor vendors used this unconventional maneuver to further their own interest by paying some big bucks into Velvet Turtle's banquet account which was then transferred on into the coffers of the corporation. Of course, they wanted to influence the restaurant manager to purchase their line of liquor. Not illegal, but apparently in violation of liquor control rules. The mystery is who knew what, and when did they know it? I don't know if Wally was even aware of the transaction, but I do know Wally did not personally enrich himself and yet he became Saga's scapegoat. He had to resign and so ended the saga of Wally, a man in command of his craft—building and managing restaurants. Shame!

I'm getting ahead of myself, but Wally and his successful operation were a big part of the reason I took my first visit to Saga. I was impressed with the ambiance of the Velvet Turtles, investigated the ownership, and so became aware of Saga corporation.

One look at the Saga offices and I was smitten. I don't know why that was so important to me, but it was. I called their location "The Campus." The site was in Menlo Park, California, and it overlooked San Francisco Bay. The one- and two-story buildings were separated by large expanses of green. It was spectacular! I felt there had to be a pony in there somewhere.

People who could build such an office complex had to have a great enjoyment of beauty and feelings for the overall environment. I don't know who romanced whom, but the beginning negotiations went smoothly. My agent negotiated with their attorneys and they arrived at a stock-for-stock transaction as a tax-free exchange which did work well for both parties. I would continue to run the Black Angus Company. I remember meeting the president of the restaurant group, Jim Morrell, who was also executive vice president of Saga. I think I've gotten that right, but who really cares—titles are boring anyway. Jim was a class act, and given that setting, I just wanted to know where to sign. Dorothy Parker

Saga Headquarters in Menlo Park, California
Photos don't do "the campus" justice.

describes "class" as "grace under pressure." Like any marriage, we had some pressured-packed times.

The merger for stock would take a few months, and before the final transfer, I was scheduled to meet the three founders. Bill Scandling, "Hunk" Anderson, and "Willy the Lock" Laughlin had met shortly after the conclusion of World War II. They were three students at Hobart College, in Geneva, New York, and it was there that they started a college feeding program, in 1946 or thereabouts, because they were confident they could put out better food than what they were getting at Hobart. I was eager to meet them because I was amazed that three young guys could start such a business and remain equal in the power structure as it grew into a large corporation. I had heard they rotated the offices of chairman, president, and vice chairman without one wielding more power than the other two—surely an outstanding example of male bonding!

Jim Morrell's assistant, John Weaver, guided me around the campus to visit each founder's office. First I met Bill Scandling who appeared to be quite cool with his slicked-back hair and neatly knotted tie. His office reflected his dress and personality. It was one of those beautiful offices where you imagined, if you moved, something might go horribly wrong. And when somebody's dressed that neatly, it makes you feel like your zipper's at half-mast and there's a spot on your tie. I'm sure my pants were closed and my tie was clean, but I had a long way to go. He appeared bored by the meeting and I thought the merger could be in trouble. First impressions can be misleading and I should know better. In the end, he was almost the savior of Saga. ALMOST!

Next in my little odyssey was Hunk Anderson who was married to a woman called "Moo." (I had to meet someone with such an unusual name and when I did, it was a pleasure. She didn't at all fit the image I first had.) From the name Hunk, I figured I'd be meeting a compatriot—a big fellow cowboy who might even have a little Swede in him. Outside of the butch haircut, Hunk didn't fit my image at all. He was neither large nor a cowboy. He had that look of "Who passed gas?" on his face. I later learned that expression disguised his basic intelligence.

Here again his office was spacious and full of stuff I eventually found out was modern art in the extreme. It looked like he was in the process of moving. I once asked him to attend our Western Experience Sale at the ranch where we sold registered cattle alternately with Western or American art. He peered at me as if I'd called him a dirty name. He said, "Are you kidding—Western art? That's not art to me." That hurt. He also appeared bored, but therein lies my fascination with first impressions—they're not worth a damn!

Last of the three, but certainly not least, was Bill Laughlin, known as "Willy the Lock." Everything about this office had a massive feeling, if you know what I mean. A huge desk and furniture you sink down into, all very intimidating. Each office was totally different, but all of them quite large, as if keeping a balance between the founders. The man behind the desk appeared to be wearing his pajamas. I was overdressed here. In time I discovered he always wore loud, way-out clothing. No butch cut or slicked-back hair here—zippo! Next I noticed another large item—a huge dog lying in front of the desk. Being an old rancher, I love dogs and I always had a least two following me around the ranch. But I'd never seen a dog in an office on a business day. I felt I might've been able to ride my horse into this interview.

Willy was not bored. He seemed fascinated by what he was saying. He was the marketing man of the group, which was an asset to the trio, but like some marketing men I know, he could be a loose cannon. AND, like other marketing men I know, he was a bit of a name dropper.

One time, while attending one of those frequent team-building sessions at some California resort complex, we broke for the day and moved out to the lawn. What captured the eyes of all of us was a huge tiger—a live, king-sized tiger—lying on the grass and attached to a way-too-small chain leash. We all approached with

Saga founders guarding the entrance to "the campus"
Left to right, Bill Scandling, Bill Laughlin and Hunk Anderson.

caution and circled the animal, even though his trainer was off to one side. What the hell was this all about? Go back to your jobs and be a tiger! Willy's idea. Anyone who thinks up things like that can't be all bad. I was impressed! It was an image you're not likely to forget.

All in all, the founders—all three of them—had obviously accomplished much and created quite an organization. It was my feeling that since they were entrepreneurs and not MBAs, they'd allow me to run my business as I saw fit. If they were bored with my accomplishments, all the better. They were basically contract feeders, which is almost opposite to restaurant feeding. We all wanted happy customers but achieved our results from different directions. I never worked closely with any of the three gentlemen, to my regret. We did mix a bit socially, but they were in Menlo Park and I was way off in Seattle. I was free to continue to run my corporation the way I wanted and that was just fine with me.

I believe they had a lot of confidence in Jim Morrell. He didn't know the restaurant business per se, but Jim was aware of that, which was a good start. He was a quick study and an asset to management of the Black Angus and Saga. The deal was done. Right after the formal signing of all the merger papers and the exchange of stock, John Weaver turned to me and said, "You are now a millionaire many times over." I replied, "I hear you, but it hasn't really sunk in yet—guess I need a break in Hawaii for a few days."

While lying on the beach in Honolulu, I made over a million dollars. Following the announcement in the Wall Street Journal, our stock moved up on the board. "Celebrate the moment of your life," as they say, but it was not meant to be. There isn't much thrill in success unless one has been close to failure—read on.

Yesterday, when I was young, I wanted just two things. One was to grow up, and the second was to be a millionaire. I had now achieved one ambition, but still have yet to accomplish the other.

It was paper profit and that's all it was. I traded my shares of stock in my twelve corporations for the shares of Saga stock on the Over-the-Counter Market (soon to move to the New York Stock Exchange). This transaction qualified as a tax-free trade, or pooling of interest, and I was now holding stock worth close to ten million dollars with no more personal debt.

It was the early seventies. As part of the agreement, I had the right to go to the market with my stock offering and obtain a considerable amount of taxable cash. I timed the offering to coincide with the presidential election of 1972 because I felt Nixon's victory would create a favorable climate for my offering. I had selected my brokerage house (Merrill Lynch) and was ready to go.

Then I made a crucial mistake.

Willy (Bill Laughlin, one of the founders) asked me if he could join in my private underwriting to get some needed cash and also bring in his brokerage house (Smith Barney). He and his broker had a large block of stock—some one hundred thousand shares—which would almost double the size of my offering. I thought about his request for too brief a period, and then remembering the good deal they had given me, said, "What the hell, go for it!" Bad move!

According to my advisers, the market read this new offering as the founders cutting out. They saw the names Laughlin and Anderson and took that to mean that two of the three Saga founders were dumping a considerable amount of stock. They confused me with Hunk Anderson.

Despite the market moving up with the election result, our stock started a free-fall. Day after day it dropped a little more—from a stock price of $28 1/2 to $17 in two months, then down to $12. The offering was postponed and then finally canceled by me. Willy withdrew his hundred thousand shares, but it was too late. By the way, the overall market continued to move up during this same time period. If you can't run with the big dogs, stay on the porch!

I decided to forget about the stock market and go to work building restaurants.

CHAPTER 6

THE GUY WHO CAME IN
FROM THE COLD

They were a great source of income and at the same time a terrible source of irritation. From the title of this chapter you probably know what I'm talking about—the restaurant coatrooms. It was years ago that we eliminated them from our design. Despite the tipping income, they were a pain in the ass for both the operator and the customer.

In the colder climates, the tips were substantial, and all we had to do was baby-sit their coats for an hour or two. We, as operators, hated them because of the frequent loss or exchange of a coat or hat. The quickest way to lose a customer was to give him or her the wrong garment (unless it was nicer than the one checked—but it never was). Lawsuits were threatened, we purchased new hats and coats, and then insurance companies started to drop us like hot potatoes. It was the custom to split the tips between the coatroom attendant and the restaurant. Sometimes some sharp gal would pay a flat fee for the concession. You can imagine how involved it could get determining half the tips or what the concession was worth. These varied greatly with the number of customers and the weather outside.

One time, to encourage an up-and-coming manager to move to a store way out into the cold boondocks, I offered him, in addition to his regular pay, the income from the coatroom. Years later, he would confide how profitable those days had been. I won't mention his name because I don't know whether the IRS got their end of the business.

, Because of the tremendous difference in volume of customers throughout the day and night, the coatrooms were not manned at all times. In the late afternoon, the counter would remain open and we would hang a sign saying, "Not Responsible for Lost Articles." Yo! That sign didn't mean squat. They were still going to sue or never come back.

We had an unusually large loss of articles at one particular store—day and night. Somebody was making a living ripping us off. None of the employees had a view of the front door or the coatroom. I contacted a friend and well-known private eye, Ward Keller. He had the idea of rigging this coat hanger. When you took the weight off the arms of this hanger, it triggered an almost invisible wire drilled through the wall, which led to a red bulb set up in the bar. As bait I used my cashmere coat. It was handsome, light tan, and fairly new, and we knew it would be the first one picked. Ward and I ordered a couple of martinis and all we could do was stare at that dumb bulb. A big snore! We were cut out of the loop with the others in the bar and felt kind of ridiculous just staring at our little invention. Of course, we hadn't told anyone about it. After two drinks, we decided to call one of his operatives to take over and we went out to look for something better to do.

When we returned a few hours later, we looked into the coatroom. The coat was gone and the hanger bars had been sprung and my first thought was, "Oh good, we've got somebody and now we can end these losses." We couldn't wait to get into the bar and find out who they'd caught. Was it a regular customer or someone I knew? I was hoping it wasn't the latter; regardless, I couldn't wait to get my hands on this guy for all the grief he'd caused us.

We walked into the bar. The light was on and the operative was sitting in a booth slurring words and trying to charm a couple of lookers. He wasn't quite sure where he was but he was having a goooood time. He had totally forgotten why he was there. All this work we did to build and disguise the trap was in vain. We never did catch the person and I never saw my coat again. Oh, the agony of defeat! The good news was that Ward never sent me a bill. He even gave me a ride in his private plane and flew me all over the Seattle area. Big deal—I would rather have had my coat back.

Another coatroom in another store almost ruined Christmas. One Christmas Eve afternoon, three of us decided we had better go shopping for our wives. We were at that stage in our marriages where we felt like going to the equivalent of Frederick's of Hollywood or Victoria's Secret. All of us spent an embarrassing hour and finished our duty with three or more beautifully wrapped flimsies and headed back to the bar. I took my presents to my office, Bob took his with him to the bar, and Ed put his in the coatroom.

The bar was jumping. Christmas Eve day used to be a huge bar day. That's not the case nowadays, and though the business is missed, that's okay because this way is better for families, marriages, and Christmas.

After a quick drink we all headed for home, but not before we heard Ed let out a yelp. His presents were missing from the unattended coatroom and he looked like he was about to cry. Too late now—all the stores were closed. Bob and I decided to do the only civilized thing we could do—we each donated one of our boxes. The only problem was, we forgot our wives weren't the same sizes and personal notes had been placed inside. We were now a little short on gifts and it didn't make for a perfect Christmas. Ed's problem was even tougher. We're not sure how he handled it, but I do remember he didn't want to talk about it.

On another Christmas Eve, in that same coatroom, one of our vendors had left two beautiful fruit baskets. One had a tag "To Stu" and the other "To Bruce," my senior vice president. They were from our fruit and produce supplier. I quickly moved mine to the office and I notified Bruce Attebery that his was waiting in the coatroom.

A short while later, my attorney, Dick Dameyer, dropped by and gave me an unexpected Christmas gift. (Maybe all those legal fees had created some guilt!) I deftly removed my name from the basket and presented it to him as his gift from me. Sure! About a week later, Bruce showed me a card he'd discovered at the bottom of his basket. It said, "Bruce, we hope you enjoyed the fruit and thank you for the business over the years." My, oh, my, did I blow that one! I waited for the repercussions, but they never came. I finally had to ask Dick about it. He never saw the card. He'd presented the gift I'd given him, with his own card, to the late Senator Henry Jackson. I could just hear the Senator saying, "Who the hell is Stu?"

The hell with coatrooms. What does the guy who came in from the cold do now? For one thing, hats aren't worn much anymore and expensive furs aren't as popular. If the truth be known, I really don't care what the guy does! It's not my problem.

DOOR NO. 1, 2, OR 3?

Behind the scenes of the restaurant you patronize are some more doors. Which door do you choose—1, 2, or 3? A lot of those names they choose for you are dumb and dumber.

> Bucks or Does
> Braves or Squaws
> His or Hers
> Shielas or Blokes
> Buoys or Gulls
> Pointers or Setters
> Birdies or Bogies
> Cocks or Hens

Then there are the pictures or cute plaques of various males and females dressed in cute clothes. Do you always know which door to choose? We're not talking brain surgery here, but you've got to admit, some operators ought to be horsewhipped.

When I remodeled my first restaurant, the men's room had splashed across the mirror: "Here's where Anderson ran out of cash." It was true. I figured I couldn't make any money in there anyway. Do you see the handwriting on the wall? Then you've visited my first john. I asked a favorite couple of mine how they met and he said he got her phone number off the men's room wall. She didn't take kindly to him telling us this story. What is it that happens to guys when they get into a public restroom? They seem to go bananas with the old pen or pencil—"boink" this and that—then they tear the toilet-paper holder off the wall. I hate to tell you this, but in some areas, women do grafitti too. It isn't pretty. It's a good thing women don't get to see the things said on men's restroom walls and vice versa.

If you've had a chance to visit the john in any rest stop along the interstate in this great country, you know they're built like the inside of a tank. We didn't have to go to that extreme in our restaurants, but close to it. We tried to make it classy—every damn surface we could we put in tiles, which are pretty tough to write on. Expensive, but better than all the things we tried including hanging the daily sports page over the urinals or installing a chalk board replete with chalk. Let them go wild. Every day the chalk was gone. They even put stupid words on the signs we placed on the wall, which said, "All employees will wash their hands before returning to work."

Just as an aside—I really got a chuckle out of the Jerry Seinfield TV program where the chef joins Jerry in the men's room, does his duty, and then tells Jerry he's going to fix him his special, as he walks out without washing his hands. You can pretty much figure there goes the old appetite. As Julia Child said on nouvelle cuisine, "It's so beautifully arranged on the plate, you know someone's fingers have been all over it."

The tiling of the restrooms is not required by local ordinances, but the proper number of plumbing fixtures is. Often local ordinances require you to do something stupid and you have to do it or you're toast. The women's john, for example, should have twice as many fixtures as the men's room. But they never think of that. How many times have we seen women standing outside waiting to get in?

YESTERDAY . . . WHEN I WAS YOUNG

As you know, Army life wasn't full of too many choices. I was a tank driver in the Eleventh Tank Battalion, Tenth Armored Division, Third Army. This was early winter in France during World War II, so not too cozy. This traveling tank had no john. In an encampment, tents were set up. We all shared so many bathrooms and showers in the service—I never did get totally comfortable with it. Our batallion was moving toward the front line. We no longer parked our tanks in a row or side by side as was our custom. For defensive reasons we spread out haphazardly all over this pasture in northern France for the night, and I remember this incident well.

At daybreak we saw this long ditch stretching through the pasture. That was it—our bathroom. Somehow this john, such as it was, had been dug during the night and it was our job to figure out how to use it this cold and snowy morning—doing our duty without dignity. There I was, poised, when I recognized a buddy, Bob Weidenbenner, from school—the Army Specialized Training Program (ASTP) at the University of Georgia. We were just starting to visit when we heard the scream of incoming mail, so we ran with the rest of them, pulling ourselves together as we ran.

How does your garden grow? Pretty good on that French pasture, I'll bet.

Our tank was the third tank to cross the Moselle River, but once across, we were allowed to pull to the side and let a constant stream of armored equipment get ahead of us on the point. What a comforting sight that was. Later that day, a bunch of Army trucks came looking more like a circus convoy than fighting apparatus.

They came into our pasture and set up tent after tent. What the hell were they doing? I noticed the troops were all black. Integration at that time was just talked about and not practiced. It was an odd-looking structure they'd erected. What could they be? Eventually the word got passed around—showers! Oh, happy day!

We got very excited since we'd all gone over two weeks without one. We didn't even mind that the water was lukewarm and we only had two minutes. Those guys weren't fooling. In two minutes they shut the water off, and you didn't want to be left all soaped up. There was a catwalk above the showers and those black soldiers kept yelling "Move it! Move it! Move it! Get your ass outta there or they'll be calling you soapy." They could yell all they wanted— I've never had a shower that did more good. Now we could put up with each other a while longer inside that tank.

One of my favorite bathroom stories, though, involves a letter I got from a lady I didn't know. The gist of the letter was as follows:

"Dear Stuart,

"Thank you, thank you, thank you! Thank you for my new sofa, new coffee table, new lamps, and new carpet."

(My wife opened the letter and was pretty nervous after the first few sentences, wondering what I'd been up to.)

The letter went on, "Let me explain. My husband went to sit down on the toilet in your restaurant, and because the seat was broken, he fell sideways and injured himself. All of the above items were purchased from the settlement we received from your corporation . . . ."

That story reminds me of my good friend, Linda Harrison, who claims that every man is born with a book that tells them how to behave and to do the "right thing" with the opposite sex. Some examples for all you women out there:

Just so you know there's a legitimate reason, Rule #5 in the Male Manual tells men not to put the toilet seat down when finished.

Rule #3 tells them not to ask directions no matter how lost they are. Why do you think Moses wandered around the desert for forty years?

Rule #16 forbids them to pick up their socks and put them in the dirty-clothes hamper. Men must leave their clothes where they fall when removed.

Rule #6 gives men full control of the TV remote. Women may be allowed to use it, but only if there's nothing on it that the male wants to watch.

Rule #14 teaches men to be able to do absolutely NOTHING. This one especially drives women crazy.

Rule #15 encourages patience. If a man needs something but there's no one around, he has only to be patient and someone will come through the room to get whatever it is he desires. No need to get up from his comfortable position, no matter what the reason.

The list goes on, but you get the idea.

I figure I've spent millions of dollars on johns over the years, so I know of what I speak. I'll bet you can guess where I spent most of our money on our newly remodeled home. Right! I've got a bathroom to die for. Steam shower with a foot Jacuzzi, TV with remote, lots of books, thick wall-to-wall carpet, a sky-lighted cathedral ceiling, wonderful art, and yes, even some beautiful tile. I deserve it! I call my room "Door No. 3," and there better not be anyone writing on the wall.

Have you about had it with bodily functions and the rooms built for same? One more experience and we'll move on.

There's a fascinating men's room in a club in California, but I'd best not tell you specifically where it is because you'll go there for all the wrong reasons. After dinner there one night, I went to the john, and when I stepped up to the urinal, a light beam was apparently triggered because a life-sized, scantily-clad, beautiful woman came "alive" on the wall smack in front of me. She was

Door No. 3

peering down at what I pulled out, commenting on what a dandy I had. That did it! Some video! I was so embarrassed, there was no way anything was going to happen after that. I tried the next stall and the same thing happened. It was just a little much.

You can now close the doors.

CHAPTER 7

THE CHARLIE
AND ERNIE SHOW

We were s-s-s-smokin'!

From the first twelve Black Angus Restaurants (all originally someone else's, with names like Double Joy, The Polynesian, The Gaslight, The Hideaway, and so forth), we now approached forty-two stores and all the new ones were "built-to-suit." This means a landowner would build a restaurant to our specifications and lease it to us. We were moving throughout the West and our future looked as bright as our past. Having moved into Canada, we became international and were grossing over one hundred million dollars a year. It was about this time in our expansion that I realized I shouldn't be so complacent. Change was coming.

While visiting down on the campus with one of the Saga founders, Bill Laughlin, I mentioned that each opening seemed better than the last and used the old slogan, "If it ain't broke, don't fix it!" He came unglued and said, "That's the worst view a progressive businessman can have!" I was surprised at the intensity of his reaction.

I was concerned because, to me, the idea of changing things just for the sake of changing them is ridiculous, especially in the restaurant business. If you're satisfying the customer, stay with it. I don't mean you shouldn't refine your formula and adapt to changes in the marketplace. In this business, do not anticipate change; instead, stay close to what your customers and employees want. Talk to your servers to find out what the customer is saying. They have the closest contact. Ask the dishwasher to report any large amounts of uneaten food he's throwing away—usually a sign it's not making the grade. Allow for customer comments on the back of the sales ticket and read them. Your customer count is your health thermometer. This count should be available every day from your cash register printout, which shows how many meals you sold. It fluctuates with the weather, new competition, and so forth, but pay attention to it.

We also calculated, on a weekly basis, the almost one hundred items on the menu according to percentage of sales. Some items would rank fifteen percent, some five and some less than one percent. We usually dropped the bottom item, replacing it with a new one we felt might sell better. That was our extent of fixing it. I was ready to argue with him, and then I figured, "What the hell?"

Trends are a different subject and they can move in fast. Early on, when I placed my liquor order for the week, I got a case of gin and one bottle of vodka. I could barely keep up with the switch as it went to a case of vodka and one bottle of gin. In those first years, it was always a shot of whisky and a water or Coke back. Now you hardly ever see a shot glass or hear the order "water-back."

A more dramatic trend is how lunch habits have changed. Many of us used to enjoy the two-hour martini lunch, which has pretty much gone by the wayside. Maybe that's not all bad, but I missed the business. I also was known to participate personally in this institution. What caused the downfall of the leisurely lunch and could we have seen it coming? Yes. The enforcement of drunk-driving laws has greatly affected our serving alcohol to patrons and their consumption of same, and that's a good change. Tax deductions for business entertainment aren't in favor anymore either. On top of that, there's been a lot of corporate down-sizing (an ugly word). Employees have to cover more territory now, so lunches have become fast-track meals. You have to stay on top of this trend or lose good customers.

Then there are adaptations—not trends, but wants and desires we must adapt to. For instance, when we went into the San Francisco area, we found that sourdough bread was a must. Our ranch bread had to go. In the town of Santa Maria, California, the pressure was on to serve their famous salsa with the beef. We accommodated them. In the city of Tacoma, Washington, we were requested to serve the noon martinis in coffee cups. We didn't accommodate those people. That wasn't an adaptation, it was just a sneaky ploy caused by a strict employer—these executives didn't want him to know they enjoyed a martini at lunch.

The above are examples of going with the flow—making no big changes, just small refinements. What was about to happen to Saga was a stunning development. This great corporation, which was well conceived and well managed, was about to turn everything upside down, with emphasis on down. To this day, I believe its eventual demise came about because of a deep-seated need to **fix it—broken or not.** Speaking as one risk taker to another—you know who you are—this business can get boring. When things are going too smoothly, we have a tendency to start something new or try to "fix" what we have. A good example was my venture into a new seafood restaurant, Stuart's at Shilshole. It came out great but only because the waterfront property increased so much in value.

The founders were doing more than a competent job with their rotation of the top positions, and the stock market reflected this. They were certainly not of retirement age, so why did they do what they did—which was to step aside? They brought in the Charlie and Ernie show—starring two new bosses, Ernest C. Arbuckle and Charles A. Lynch. Ernie became the new chairman of the board. He'd previously been chairman at Wells Fargo Bank and before that dean of the business school at Stanford. He certainly had a strong background, but I don't believe he'd ever seen the inside of a bar. Next came Charlie (Looking-for-a-Few-Good-Yes-Men) Lynch as the new president of Saga. He came from the Grace Corporation and a few other companies before that. As far as I could tell, he didn't know diddley about marketing or the restaurant business. Were these two gentlemen—a statistician and a banker—to be the guiding lights of a free-wheeling, independent, swinging restaurant business? But why?

Why indeed! From the standpoint of the people involved with the operation of the chain, we were generally very pleased with our relationship with the founders, the other divisions, and particularly with the Saga personnel with whom we dealt directly. The corporation was strong and the financial community was an indicator this.

President Charlie was busy at the Menlo Park offices for the first two years and our contact was primarily limited to a hello at company meetings. At the point where my company had opened seventy restaurants, Charlie and I had a confrontation.

What provoked this conflict was the promotion of my number one gal, "The Iron Butterfly," Bobbi Loughrin, to assistant vice president of administration and I notified Saga after the fact. Charlie became "absolutely infuriated" (to quote him) with this move. I got my dander up because I thought his tirade reflected his opposition to my appointing the first female vice president. At all the meetings I went to at Saga with all the top suits, never had there been a woman in attendance. I never had a notification system for approval of the other four vice presidents. This looked like trouble, and I wanted to stand on principle. The new Chairman Ernie asked if I would drop by his office at the Menlo Park campus. He started with: "I don't think the conflict between you and Charlie is all that great. The two of you have really just started to relate to each other and you should bide your time on this issue. Give Charlie a little time and the two of you will work well together."

His attitude toward me was conciliatory and it certainly put me in a mood to cooperate. It was getting to that time when I was to meet with Charlie and the days dwindled down to a precious few. I discussed the pending confrontation with Bobbi. She said, "Please, Stuart, don't make me an issue. I don't want it to come to

Charlie and Ernie

that." I also felt this was a battle I was doomed to lose. I'd been around much longer and was in charge of the fastest-growing and most profitable division in the company, but I had the feeling the founders and the board of directors would back their new president if it came down to that. So I apologized for not going through channels and let my ego deflate. That's all right; he could've fired my ass.

Bobbi kept her title, her raise, and attended the Black Angus executive committee meetings with the vice presidents. I remember at the first one I asked her to get us coffee and realized immediately what I was doing. She was not a token female. Shame on me! We all got our own coffee, as it should've been.

Another confrontation with Charlie was a discussion that became somewhat tense and we both started quoting Peter Drucker, the business guru, as if there were two Peters. Charlie said, "The last thing you do is build your organization around people." I said, "I perceive the Black Angus chain as one that was built around people."

I'd say without a doubt that my greatest asset in the business world was my ability to find and select individuals with great talent for the restaurant industry. I had methods that are best described by the saying: "Fit the coat to the man, not the man to the coat." In other words, when you find an outstanding individual, find a position somewhere so he or she can become part of your group or family.

For example, one evening, while working late in my office, a young man came in to sell me some advertising in a ski magazine. I had zero interest in placing an ad for my two stores, but I was a ski bum, so I started working with him on trade-outs and swaps. While we talked, something else was happening. His personality and sincerity appealed to me, so I asked him about his current job. Dead end. His name was David Rollo. He went on to be our personnel director, and he inspired us all before he died at the age of forty-two.

David Rollo

Left to right: The Black Angus Executive Committee: Ron Stephenson, Haig Cartozian, Tom Lee, Bobbi Loughrin, and Bruce Attebery. From Saga: Jim Morrell, Dan Sharpley, and Ralph Pica, with me in the middle

It was my privilege to give the eulogy at the memorial service for David. Let me share with you some of my remembrances so maybe you can know him a little.

If there is a heaven—and I believe there is—David's there and I'll bet he's asking a lot of questions. We all smile in our remembering, and that's the way he'd have wanted it. I liked his style, his manner, his straightforward approach to a new proposal, and he was from Spokane where we were getting ready to open our third restaurant. By the time he left that dark afternoon, after two or three hours, I had hired him as an assistant manager at the Spokane store. He loved to tell the story of when I sent him there. I forgot to tell the manager, Bruce Attebery, that he was coming. I would love to have witnessed that confrontation. It was always easy to relate to David because he was never devious. Those who didn't know him well suspected him to be naive. It was just that he was uncommonly direct and had such a trusting nature. His honesty and loyalty were superb and his great laugh was contagious. David, I'm glad you stopped by that afternoon many years ago.

David is just one case of finding those outstanding individuals who might come along from any field of endeavor. The vice president of southern operations, Tommy Lee, was a top sergeant in the Army looking for part-time work. He started as a bar-back. Not a big man, but big enough to handle two bullies trying to give me a bad time in the bar one night. Vice president of development Ron Stephenson was a coffee salesman calling on me. Haig Cartozian, the vice president of marketing, was a Navy officer who offered to share his table with my foursome at the crowded Seattle Yacht Club after a football game. Bruce Attebery you've already met. I'm the smartest of all because I always hired smarter people than I.

There wasn't time to discuss all my great hiring abilities with Charlie, but I kept thinking back on these stories as I heard him in the background of my mind assuring me that I had not demonstrated the "complete businessman's competence" in running a hundred million dollar-plus chain. However, he then gave me credit for running the best dinner-house operation in the country. Explain that to me!

Who won? Don't ask me—I don't know. I've heard it said, "To always get the last word in when arguing, just say okay."

Who had the last word? First, last, and always—Charlie!

Not to make a plan is planning for failure. The plan! The plan! It caused panic every year, and at times it became an exercise in futility. Charlie would set the master plan by projecting how many millions he needed to surpass the previous year's results by a healthy fifteen percent, regardless of the reality of the situation. After running it by the board of directors for their automatic stamp of approval, the dollars in the plan were split up among the divisions through some formula that no one understood. We, the Black Angus officers, would massage our portion of the plan and resubmit it based on a realistic increase but always somewhat less than the percent Charlie was asking. Back it would come. His charts and graphs somehow gave him what he needed to impress the financial community.

The following must die just between us, but we didn't knock ourselves out because we knew the five-year plan was really a one-year plan and the yearly plan was a six-month plan. Planning is an important tool in business, but the way this one worked was overkill. You need to understand the service business. It's not manufacturing. Not at all. Anyone who tells you business is business and it's all the same hasn't been there. However, the plan had a positive side. It made us study and push our figures around and get to know them like we should. We all learned a great deal from the plan even though we cussed it constantly. We spent more time on the plan than doing the things that would get us where the plan said we should be. Does that make any sense?

Then there were the charts and graphs. We didn't call Charlie "Charts" Lynch without good reason. Here was a life and a management style that revolved around a graft or a chart. Our division was just one big chart to Charlie and he couldn't see past that wiggly line.

Just when peace reigned over the battleground, here came another biggy. See where you stand on this one. When do you designate an heir to your throne—or, should I ask, do you even designate an heir? Charlie wanted me to name the person who would assume my position when I moved on or out. I was reluctant because I had a smooth-working executive committee of four vice presidents, soon to be five. I didn't want to lose any one of them, and that is a possibility when they become aware they're not "it." I just didn't want to make that decision.

There's another factor to consider. I mentioned my greatest asset, so it's only fair to mention my biggest liability. I procrastinate! I wasn't aware of this fact until my cohorts, on several different occasions, pointed it out. My response was: "It's a method to develop responsibility in others." Bullshit! I was rationalizing and I knew it. To procrastinate can be a very bad habit. I knew I needed to work on it, but I could never decide when. I still can't. I used to say, "They don't remember how long it took you to make a decision but how well that decision was made." More bullshit.

As it turned out, I stood by my decision not to make a decision, and I won that one against Charlie because I never did designate an heir. By the way, Charlie never designated an heir for his position.

None of us knew it at the time, but this corporation only had a few more years before it passed into the land of memories.

PART II

RAISING BEEF

(ON THE RANCH)

CHAPTER 8

THE EYES AND EARS
OF THE WORLD

Our world—the small world of Black Angus—was driven by the magic of the tube, the big eye of television. But I started with the ears, the radio in the Seattle market area. I didn't have enough money to purchase time, so instead I worked out a trade with local deejays. They could eat and drink on me in exchange for a few on-the-air plugs from them. It helped me and they had fun swinging with the crowds. It was a win-win situation.

As more restaurants were opened, our marketing became more sophisticated. Haig Cartozian became the genius behind the so-called "Beef Baron," "Steak King," and "Corporate Cowboy" image—all referring to me, the star. It wasn't done with smoke and mirrors, and therein lies the fascination.

James J. Hill of the Great Northern Railroad, which happened to border my ranch for miles, made this classic statement:

"Most men who have really lived have had, in some shape, their great adventure. This railroad is mine."

Well, the ranch was mine. The Black Angus Cattle Company Ranch, purchased by me in 1966, was comprised of twelve hundred acres in Eastern Washington, ten miles west of Ellensburg (the actual address was Thorp). This was my fourth and last ranch. As time went on I added more cattle range by purchase and lease (Quillicine Range) to where I ended up with twenty-six hundred deeded and twenty-two thousand leased acres. Now I could raise cattle and continue to satisfy part of the beef needs of the restaurants. However, as the chain grew it became impractical to furnish the beef. Only twenty-two percent of the animal is used and that leaves seventy-eight percent to get rid of some way or other. I tried trading the parts of the carcass that we didn't use for steaks and roasts, but it became too involved, so we dropped the practice of furnishing beef. We then developed very strict specifications for the restaurant beef and primarily worked with one company to purchase our meat.

This property became a studio for television productions. It was the real thing—dust, dung, and the sounds of the great outdoors. Not only did I raise cattle on a grand scale, I had created a stage in the process. A river runs through it (the Yakima), as do two major railroads—the Milwaukee and Great Northern—and it's bordered by Interstate 90. The potential was there for making TV ads, throwing large private and charitable parties, flying lighter-than-air craft, and raising magnificent black Clydesdales (our parade draft horses) and Black Angus show cattle.

People are always fascinated with the Wild West, and Haig and I took every advantage of the association. One may remember the ads that depicted the entire restaurant crew marching through the ranch in their uniforms, carrying plates of sizzling steaks, or the helicopter that landed me and my ranch manager at the silos, which were emblazoned with our logo, where we hopped aboard a Jeep and took off to tour the ranch. Or how about one television skit we did in a chill room at a local packing house? I walked by the meat which was hanging there and patted its rump twice to signify it was "choice." I got a complaint letter from a TV viewer saying it was a sexist action. I had a little trouble handling that beef!

The tube drew many types of comments, mostly favorable, and we found it to be a powerful medium. Not only that but the commercials were fun, and I could do my "outstanding" acting

In tuxedos, me, Bruce Attebery and Ron Stephenson — 1971
It's that-a-way to the office.

A couple of early ads we ran using the ranch and the vice presidents.

Me in 1971 with ex-wife Edie—dining with "the girls"

within sight of my house. Not many performers can say that. Andy Warhol says every man has fifteen minutes of fame. I did approximately thirty, 30-second commercials. Do the math.

We also had hot-air balloons which always created quite a stir but came with a different set of problems. To put it mildly, cattlemen don't have any great love for those huge monsters. It was a thrill to fly over the beautiful Kittitas Valley with a chase car keeping an eye on us. Being a productive valley, it was hard to find a suitable spot to land. We usually had to float farther than we wanted to in order to avoid the crops and livestock. It's a grand experience and the silence is only disturbed by the occasional necessity of firing a little more gas when the balloon drifts too low. You have to be ready for that blast of propane because it'll shake you out of your reverie. It'll also shake up any livestock below you. When you pull the cord, the cattle look up to see where the noise is coming from and then, when they see that big thing hanging overhead, all hell breaks loose. One cattleman I know even threatened to "shoot the damn stupid thing down." I've seen cattle and horses go right through barbed wire fences.

I wasn't even in the basket on our most momentous balloon show. I was attending a football game between the Washington Huskies and the Stanford Indians at Stanford. There was a quarterback there with the now-familiar name of Elway and he hurt our Huskies—bad! I don't remember much more than that, and for good reason.

All three of our balloons were going to fly over the stadium at half time. It would be a fantastic promotion. What I didn't know was how close to the stadium's top edge they would be. Our seats were near that edge and suddenly I heard the familiar sound of the gas being released. We all jumped about a foot out of our seats as that balloon sailed just a few feet above us. If you've never been close to a hot-air balloon you can't appreciate how huge they are and how loud the noise of that gas burning is. In about ten minutes, here came the second one—even closer—

One of the "fleet" giving rides at the ranch party barn.

The magnificent black Clydesdale hitch—the gentle giants

Are they watching a lecture or a skit at our annual management meeting?
It's your call.

The end of the skit. I don't recognize anyone—sorry.

Have you ever tried to catch a greased pig? It's very instructive!

Our manager's version of the *Summer Games* (note our house on the hill).

and then the third one. It was quite a show. I was more worried about getting arrested than I was winning the game. Later that evening at the airport, a man recognized me and came running up and said, "I just have to ask you something. How did you get that one balloon down and back up so fast?" Come to think of it, who needs a herd of balloons?

The main reason we had them was for store openings and special events. We tried to float them near the freeway in the morning traffic on the first day of a restaurant's operation so people would take note. During the week, we gave tethered rides in the parking lot to reporters, the employees, their kids, and customers. The balloons always gave us a shot in the arm in the early weeks at a new location.

Among the more memorable functions for me were the annual company meetings attended by the headquarters' staff, district managers, and store managers—close to two hundred people. Of course each meeting had its business side, where each department head gave his or her annual report, but the part I remember most— and I believe most of the attendees do, too—was the camaraderie everyone enjoyed. We had baseball, volleyball, skits assigned to a different group each year, side-splitting donkey baseball, and a thousand more stories and events that came away from those gatherings.

Friends have asked me if I miss the ranch. I miss the cattle, the dogs, and the outdoors, but I especially miss the black Clydesdale horses. Those gentle giants were used for many a parade and store opening. It wasn't easy to find big Clydesdales, and when we limited it to black, it really became difficult. They had to be at least seventeen hands high with lots of white feathers on all hooves. Most Clydes are brown or bay such as the Anheuser-Busch eight-horse hitch which many have seen on TV commercials, but it didn't help us—wrong color. It became so difficult to locate animals that met our criteria we had to start our own breeding program. Talk about becoming attached! When we lost a couple along the way, there was real mourning involved. Even now, as I write about those huge horses, I seem to have something in my eye.

I remember many a parade where those beautiful geldings kept high-stepping for the crowd for miles, and the applause seemed to make them step even higher. Hundreds of people lining the route would rise up as we came by and you can guess what they yelled at me: "Where's the beef?" But now, parade days have passed and the horses are enjoying their new homes. Time and everything else marches on.

Publicity in the restaurant business is always worth something. Well, I suppose publicity of one kind or another could turn out negative, but fortunately we haven't experienced that yet. As for me doing my civic duties, I was always ready, willing, and able. If it served some good cause, I was all for it. I really enjoyed my time as chairman for the Washington cancer drive, grand marshal of the rodeo parade, King Neptune for the Seattle Seafair, involvement with the 4-H, WAIF, and other organizations.

As Confucius says, "If you love what you do, you will never work another day in your life."

Involvement in community affairs and charitable activities is a practice we took with us into the different areas. Our expansion plans were keyed to certain TV markets. We felt it took four or more stores to support a strong TV campaign in certain viewing areas, and that was usually the way we would go into a new city. Of course, this type of expansion also worked well when creating districts for management and supervision. So, as we moved into Denver, Phoenix, Minneapolis, San Diego, and other locales, we inundated the cities with four or more stores all within a period of months.

Does the following ring any bells? "My years as a rancher have given me the edge in selecting only the best cuts of beef for my restaurants," or ". . . and we'll do the dishes." That was the essence of my TV script for many years. Wherever I went I was expected to "do the dishes." That's the power of television. But one of the best ads was the one that said, "You've got my name on it."

Grand Marshall Stuart
Stuart was selected by the Ellensburg Rodeo Board of Directors as Grand Marshall of the 1978 Ellensburg Rodeo Parade. The parade was held on September 2 in Ellensburg, Washington.

Left to right: E.J. Zarelli, Victor Rosellini, me, Walter Clark, Dave Cohn—all recipients of the hospitality industry's "Man of the Year" award

"King Rex XXVIII of Seafair."
Commodore Haig Cartozian in the background on the left.

Ever wonder what in the hell we're doing with that long name "Stuart Anderson's Black Angus/Cattle Company Restaurants?" I'm sure a lot of you frankly don't give a damn, but believe me, those of us who had to type it out, sign it on legal papers, or pay for it in neon sure have rued the day. The use of my name identified the operation from others with the same or similar names to Black Angus or Cattle Company, but oddly enough, that's not how it got started.

Back in the early days, that long name appeared to be a shrewd move, but the value it brought has been more than offset by the electric bills for the neon lights. The first Black Angus was facing Elliott Avenue—a very busy street that was the main thoroughfare from Seattle to "Swede Town" (Ballard), a "suburb" populated mostly by Scandinavian descendants. Using my name in bright neon was a smart decision and it certainly didn't hurt my first Black Angus restaurant operation. There are almost as many Andersons in Seattle's phone book as there are Smiths. The fact that Stuart was a Scottish name told the astute customers they were patronizing a restaurant with a good bargain. It's a business fact that people support establishments of their own race or religion, perhaps a form of prejudice, pride, or reverse discrimination, but that's the way it is.

"Black Angus" came from the breed of cattle I raised. When we took the operation into the Portland, Oregon, area, we got slapped with a lawsuit over the use of the Black Angus name. We won the suit because we were the first to use the name in the Northwest. The small restaurant suing us tried again in a different court. In this case, we were ordered to use the full name "Stuart Anderson's Black Angus Restaurant" in everything we did—even how we answered the phone. I decided, to hell with it; we'll just change our name to "Cattle Company," which we were going to use in Anchorage, Alaska, anyway because of a name conflict there. The smartest thing that Portland restaurant owner could've done was ride on our successful shirttails as an operator in Vancouver, Canada, did. That guy even changed his entry to the same street as ours so people would get confused and end up in his restaurant instead. We did a lot for his business.

Here we were, doing great volume in the Beaverton area of Portland, and in one day everything changed—signs, menus, stationery, and anything else that involved the name. With great trepidation I watched customer counts and listened to hear if the employees answered the phone correctly. No problem—business stayed strong. The chain is known in Alaska, Indiana, Minnesota, Oregon, and Hawaii as "Stuart Anderson's Cattle Company Restaurant." It's the same menu, same price, and same operation. We have become the patron saint of the neon sign business and we had to have two versions of our television commercials and other advertising. But in many cases now we're just known as Stuart Anderson's Restaurant. Okay? Speaking of names . . .

YESTERDAY . . . WHEN I WAS YOUNG

After Pearl Harbor, I tried to enlist in the Army Air Force—no chance, poor depth perception. After another year at college, the draft caught up to me. I was attending the University of Southern California and it was quite a shock to go to an induction center. I'll never forget going through a physical exam in San Pedro, California, for draft board classification. You strip down and have different doctors poking and prodding you to get the okay for service. The doctor in charge, of exactly what I'm not sure, asked me what a big fixed scar on my hip was from. I'm not sure how I answered him, but I know it was wrong. I think I said osteoporosis or something like that, and he gave me a dumb look, shrugged, and sent me on down the line. Eventually, I was given my papers classifying me as 1A. Hot dog!

After basic training in Arkansas, I was given a choice of Officer Training Corps or back to college in the ASTP (Army Specialized Training Program). I opted for college and was sent to the University of Georgia for engineering courses. Because of

111

the wartime personnel demand for the looming invasion of Europe, this program didn't last too long, and we all were returned to regular service. After tank training in the South, I was sent overseas to serve in England, France and Germany. Then, after front-line duty, I was eventually shipped back to the USA and discharged in Colorado. The thrust of this story is that I should've learned how to remember and pronounce a difficult but important medical term.

When you leave the service, the Army gives you an exit physical—no charge. This time another doctor asked me what the scar on my hip was and I gave him the correct answer—osteomyelitis (bone poisoning). He looked shocked and asked me to repeat it. I did. "NO WAY!" he cried. "You must have the name wrong." I told him, "I'm sure it is, because I almost died when it came on me as a teen-ager." He said, "If that's true, you shouldn't have been in the service. Ever!"

Not remembering one word, albeit a long and confusing one to a kid, has altered my life. How it could've changed my life, I don't know—it's too much to contemplate. The high-noon excitement of those years I'll never forget—the fast pace, the unique dangers, and the guys and gals who've disappeared into the mists of time. I'm living the American dream, but what I would've missed or where I'd be now if I had been ineligible (4-F) for duty is more than I can think about right now. I'll contemplate it tomorrow. Osteomyelitis, a bone disease, has basically disappeared since the advent of penicillin. I never intended to deceive—I had honestly forgotten the name. As things have turned out, I'm glad I screwed up. It was a most momentous time of my life which I would've sorely missed if I'd remembered that word.

That's not the first name I've forgotten, nor the last, as any number of close friends can attest to. Dave Rollo, whom you met earlier, had the same difficulty with names as I did. One day he came into my office excited about a class he'd taken to improve your memory. It sounded like a class I badly needed, so I asked him the name of the school. As he struggled with the name, we looked at each other and broke up. I never pursued that class.

Advertising and the other aspects of marketing are all long-term investments in building a strong following and a favorable image in a very competitive business. The western-style marketing program, started by Haig Cartozian and me years ago, is continuing with the new management. We are all proud of the excitement our entire package created for customers and employees alike. Haig and I didn't always agree, but if we never disagreed, one of us wouldn't have been necessary.

Someone once said something like this: "Selling beef without advertising is like winking at a girl in the dark—you know what you're doing, but nobody else does."

The outdoor studio

CHAPTER 9

THEY CAME NOT TO PRAISE
THE RANCHER
BUT TO BURY HIM

THE RAPE OF THE LAND

July 20: "Grasshoppers are extremely numerous and have destroyed every species of grass from one to ten miles above the river and a great distance back."

Sept. 22: "There was little or no wood here on the river, with the exception of a few cottonwoods scattered here and there and grass was completely lacking. . . . We had to cut down three cottonwoods and make them [the horses] eat the bark."

June 27: "It is amazing how very barren the ground is between this and the Little Missouri, nothing hardly to be seen but prickly-pear cactus. Our horses are nearly starved. There is grass in the woods but none in the plains. . . ."

July 21: "It was now the dry season, which in these parts continues from the middle of July to the end of autumn. The whole prairie was dry and yellow. The least motion, even of a wolf crossing it, raised the dust. We could recognize the vicinities of the herds of buffaloes at a distance from the clouds of dust which they occasioned. All the small rivers were completely dried up."

Two of the above comments were taken verbatim from the diary of one LaRocgue, a British trader on the Powder River on June 27 and the Tongue River on September 22, 1805. That's right, over one hundred and ninety years ago. The diary entry from July 20 was taken from a Captain Clark, U.S. Army, in 1806, and the entry made on July 21 was from the German Prince Maximillian, south of Wolf Point, Montana, in 1833, some one hundred and sixty-three years ago.

Au naturel—no cattle! They hadn't been introduced to that area yet and conditions were dry, dusty, and devastating.

There was a recorded drought the year of 1805 and over twenty more have been documented since. A drought is a fact of nature, I'm sorry to say, and creates dramatic hardships on our range lands. The cattlemen also suffer during these periods, but they do not create the condition, and in almost all situations, don't add to the destruction of the land. However, guess who gets blamed despite efforts to lighten the load by reducing the number of animals on the land and shortening the grazing period? The bad conditions of the western range land have many causes, but cattle raising is not a major factor. Drought, fire, and even grass-hoppers are the main contributors to soil erosion. Nature is the handmaiden of the Lord.

The efforts of most livestock producers, range scientists, and federal land managers have improved conditions. Managed grazing gives us better grass than if the practice didn't exist. It's like mowing a lawn—the grass thickens and improves. Our cow herds survive mostly on pastures and hillsides where no crops could be cultivated for human consumption anyway. Any rancher or farmer who has land which can raise wheat, corn, or any other feed crop for human consumption will not use that land for cattle, except maybe for gleaning the fields which is a benefit to all. There's a much higher per-acre return from producing crops instead of livestock. Economics determine the best use of land, which is as it should be. The range is usually rocky ground that cannot be plowed, hillsides too steep for equipment, inaccessible mountain pastures, acreage too arid for crops, and federal lands held in perpetuity for our future. Therefore, cattle take very little from food supplies for our population and others.

The danger of disastrous forest fires in primitive lands is lessened with grazing because the grasses do not get tall enough to choke themselves off and die, leaving a tall, dry brush that will burn readily. The summer of 1996 was the worst fire season in thirty years, and anything we can do to lessen fuel loads in our forest should be considered. A couple of years back, over one million acres burned in Yellowstone National Park where cattle didn't graze. In the summer of 1966, destructive fires occurred in many areas in the West where grazing wasn't allowed. Where there had been livestock the fires were easier to control. No fuel—no fire!

On my ranch, on some of the hilly and rocky fields where we weren't able to use equipment, we used our cattle to do the job for us. To improve our pastures, we scattered seed over the ground from aircraft and sent in the cattle to trample them into the dirt. Come spring, these fields would really green up. Cattle improve the soil. It would be a very rare soil type where cows would pack it instead of aerate it. The instructions on that packet of seed you purchase will usually state "Cover the seeds with 1/2 inch of soil and/or press into the ground." Nobody does that better than cattle and their manure fertilizes the land.

Scientists working on government projects have gone one step further with this idea of seeding. They feed the cattle gelatin capsules that contain the seeds of the plants they want to establish on poor quality range land. These capsules dissolve in one of the stomachs and follow along the digestive tract, into the manure, and onto the ground. It has been found that approximately fifty percent of the seed is passed by the cattle and surrounded by the manure for a perfect seed bed. These cattle are lured to an area in need of seeding by the use of salt blocks or other methods.

If you think about what it means to nurture a renewable natural resource, you'll realize the livestock producer will respect that process for his own economic survival. He will treat that land with care and tenderness while benefiting wildlife as well. It just makes good sense. The land sustained me and I tried to manage it with great care.

A well-managed grazing program as practiced by the vast majority of cattlemen assists our range land in so many ways:

- The grass holds the soil, reducing erosion.
- The grass holds the water, allowing it to sink in instead of running off.
- The grass produces oxygen.
- Livestock break up the crusted ground so seeds can grow.
- Grazing prevents the plant's own growth from choking off new growth which comes from the plant base.
- Cattle fertilize the land.

An experienced range ecologist I met had this interesting example. He said to give him four acres. On one acre would be a Stuart Anderson Restaurant with its paved parking lot. On the second one would be a residence with a nice lawn and garden. On the third an acre of corn, and on the fourth an old range cow with her calf.

The restaurant requires lots of energy and creates waste. The standing water from rains or cleaning generates polluted run-off from the parking lot, which replaced oxygen-producing greenery. The home and garden use water and energy and leave waste and pollution, and the yard has to be fertilized, irrigated, mowed, and weeded, often with the use of a polluting power mower, herbicides, or pesticides. The acre of corn can take up to a hundred and ninety pounds of nitrogen for fertilizer (Do we know how this affects our aquifers?), may require pesticides, and uses lots of water. That old cow just keeps on renewing herself as a protein-producing resource. Her waste is excellent fertilizer for the land she's on and she doesn't need much water. It's by far the most efficient and cleanest of your choices. The most sustainable and renewable form of agriculture is grazing. Sustainable agriculture may be broadly defined as ecologically sound agriculture, or narrowly defined as eternal agriculture—that is, agriculture that can be practiced continually for eternity.

What happens when grazing is no longer allowed? Go visit the federal lands in our Southwest, particularly Zion National Park, the Painted Desert, and areas around Lake Powell where grazing has been prohibited. In less than twenty years after the grazing ban was effective this land is dying, exemplifying what happens when domesticated hoofed animals are no longer allowed. There just isn't enough wildlife to handle the job. The soil has crusted over and most seeds cannot enter. It's a tragic loss of grass that has resulted in dramatic erosion. This long-term damage to areas of the Southwest is a sad example of fuddled thinking from some of the environmental community. I hope we can learn from this, for we hold the future in our hands—or should I say in our hoofed grazers?

I've got another problem—same general subject. How about this statement? "Don't eat hamburger for a week and save an acre of rainforest in South America." I must ask, who ever started this rumor? They need to get out more often. How about some facts.

We do not import any fresh beef from South America! You can eat that hamburger with a clear conscience, and don't let the doomsayers tell you otherwise. Your best friend the dog may be eating some canned beef from a Latin American country, as we do import less than one percent (.6) which is cooked or canned. About ninety-four percent of the beef consumed in the United States is produced domestically and only six percent is imported—the majority of which is from New Zealand and Australia. There is no fresh beef from Brazil or South America that would be in any hamburger from any fast-food chain in the United States—period!

The destruction of the tropical forest is something we all hate to see. Those trees provide food and shelter to almost half of the world's species of wildlife. They are the so-called "lungs of the world," but the land underneath is not suitable to cattle raising or most farming. This soil is not what most people would expect. It's quite thin and lacking the normal nutrients needed for crops.

The rainforests shouldn't be cleared and destroyed for raising cattle, but the practice isn't discouraged by the Brazilian government.

119

We know that we, as an importing nation, are not contributing to the clearing of these forests; however, their burgeoning population certainly is. The huge trees of the rainforest are rooted in soil that couldn't grow grass long enough to sustain a ranching operation. It's an upside-down world with all the growth and vegetation on the top of the canopy. The sun and the rain penetrate slowly and the dirt is weak. It will never be very productive except for what it does now. I've seen three or four head of cattle in a green, lush pasture and they were skinny old things. What looks perfect may have no kick.

As you probably gathered, this is one case where I would agree with the environmentalists. There are five billion acres of tropical forest in the world, according to the United Nations' figures, and none of it is feasible to efficiently raise cattle. What can we do? Don't ask me, I don't know. It's not our government nor our country. Here is a situation where political elements need to get involved and regulate land use. I can't believe I said that, but this is a unique condition and "further study is needed."

Along these same lines is this: "Eat one less hamburger and save some food for the hungry and needy ones." Almost all our hamburger comes from non-fed beef. In other words, the hamburger we enjoy would be a product that comes indirectly from feed that's not edible by humans, such as grass, potato waste, and the like. The ivory-tower types who write some of these articles should be made to walk a few acres in a rancher's boots before making uninformed fools of themselves. The following is a good example.

I recently read an article that upset me because it was so lacking in fact and was so prejudicial against the ranchers. I suppose there are some fools we have to suffer gladly. King Feature Syndicate columnist, Calvin Trillin, wrote: ". . . taxpayers are subsidizing the Hewlett-Packard livestock operation." He was referring to William Hewlett and David Packard of the H-P empire, and the use of federal lands in Idaho. Oh, puh-leeze! We, the people, don't pay them to run their cattle on government land—they pay us. It's a debatable sum perhaps, but it's not a subsidy. What disturbs me is the influence the uninformed have on fragile minds. Read on and then make a decision about who's right or wrong.

Two important points to make: First, the very wealthy people of the country make up a small minority of those who rent federal land for grazing so we're talking about a tiny fraction here. There are 1.2 billion acres classified as range land—that's over half of all United States' land. Second, the taxpayers would have to pay for the functions performed by the ranchers, and considering these are beneficial for the general population and lessen government spending, why would we want to change this? The ranchers have to buy the cattle to harvest the grasses and still leave enough for the wildlife. They have to go onto the land and continuously relocate the cattle, move the salt blocks, build and maintain the fences, check on the health of the animals, develop water holes, and generally manage those federal lands, whether that area be mountains, marshes, shrub land, or desert. The wildlife benefit from the salt blocks and water holes. They do not get paid to do this—none of it. No subsidies. No tax breaks. Set your bias aside and think about how much it would cost us taxpayers to do what the ranchers now do—AND THEY PAY THE GOVERNMENT (US) TO DO IT!

> "The recipe for perpetual ignorance is:
> 'Be satisfied with your opinions and
> content with your knowledge.'"
> Elbert Hubbart

While scientists are continually measuring the health of the range land, cattle producers are constantly working to improve them. Grazed areas appear to be healthier than range that is fenced to keep out cattle. Grazing is sustainable agriculture that keeps plant life fresh, providing an ecosystem that benefits the cattle, the rancher and those who share that space. Cattle ranchers are dedicated to the care of their cattle and the land. To switch from grazing to a less productive practice makes no economic sense. One last point

I would like to make. The cattlemen who lease these lands are not in conflict with campers, fishermen, hunters, hikers, or wildlife.

May the sun shine warmly on all those who work and enjoy the range.

STUPID IS AS STUPID SAYS!

So many of us have seen the pictures of young children throughout the Horn of Africa in various stages of starvation. If you weren't moved, as I was, by those photos, I don't want to know you. We had to do something, but not what was suggested by Linda McCartney, wife of one of the Beatles. She said something like this: "If the people in the United States stopped eating meat, we could feed the world." This represents total ignorance of the world's food situation.

The famine that caused us to get involved in Somalia was created by the ancient clan system. The culture of that country is difficult to understand in our world. Starvation throughout the rural areas and consequent fighting between warlords were a side effect of the clan system. Livestock was stolen and food was hoarded as anarchy reigned over the land. One clan might have had an abundance of food it wouldn't think of sharing with the clan next door. Then you have subclans within each larger unit contributing to the havoc. The British, who colonized Somalia, granted it independence as recently as 1960. They couldn't resolve the hatreds that existed in the clan and subclan systems, so, in essence, gave up.

The United States temporarily ended the famine but failed miserably in trying to establish a central government or a fair food distribution system that could continue after we completed our role. We ran across graft, waste, unnecessary expenses, food going to the wrong people, and were able to institute only a temporary solution to the problem. Trucks delivering food to areas in need passed field after field of ample grain. Remember, famines are caused by humans while crop failures are the result of natural factors. It's interesting to note that there has never been a famine in a country that has a democratic government. We left the country of Somalia basically as we found it after two years, two billion dollars and, worst of all, American casualties. Armed militiamen still roam the countryside.

Because Africa is such a beautiful and fascinating continent, I have personally taken three trips there and found the politics, in most cases, in turmoil, so I know of what I speak. The solution is not to send them food, but there is a way to help our fellow man. The emerging countries have a great need for education, and in particular, knowledge about raising food for their own exploding population. (In Kenya the population is increasing four percent every year—more than four times our own.) It's difficult to create ample crops in an arid climate; however, we can teach them the skills to increase production using equipment loans and giving them our advanced irrigation practices and methods to minimize drought damage. What we need to export is expertise, and a little education on family planning wouldn't hurt either.

The United States produces ample food supplies. True. In fact, we have surpluses. The government even pays subsidies to some farmers not to grow crops and provides low-cost loans to others to encourage them to store their surpluses. It's not how much food is available for the world but the political and economic factors that cause the shortage problems. We live in two different worlds.

Both of the above items, the destruction of the rainforests and food situations of the world, are topics too complicated for this book about beef. Besides, I shouldn't be pontificating on problems deserving entire books on each subject. For those interested, some of the books I've read include:

1. *Geography of Famine*, by William A. Dando
2. *Hunger in History*, by Lucille F. Newman
3. *Famine; Social Crisis and Historical Change*, by David Arnold
4. *Lessons of the Rainforest*, by Kenneth I. Taylor

Helen with a native in an African village in January,1996

BRUTALIZE THE BEAST

I heard someone once say, "The life of the cow is miserable." Yeah—compared to what?

Down through the ages, man and beast have supported one another. It's hard to hug a cow, but sometimes you just feel like doing it. When we can't, the least we should do is make their life as pleasant as possible, and I believe most all ranchers work at that. Anyone who thinks otherwise doesn't know cattlemen. Do these people believe they are peering into the face of evil when they see a rancher? Get real!

Mothers, don't let your babies grow up to be cowboys, unless you own the ranch, and even then, think twice. Some environmentalists and animal rights activists will spend all their time and effort making life tougher for your cowboy, like it's not tough enough already with the hard work, hard riding, long hours, and little profit. Now compare the cowboy's life to the animals he watches over.

As you drive through the country, watch the cattle out in the fields and think on this: Pastoral settings are the stuff of famous paintings. Whether it's mountains, hills, deserts, or savannas they're a part of, cattle spend their lives in the great American outdoors. Food is always available to them, either as pasture or hauled in by the rancher. Their health is constantly looked after. They are in a social community with friends. If they have difficulty birthing, help is close by. Not only that, there's lots of good sex during breeding season.

You hear from some quarters that animals are often packed into trucks or trains at market time. Maybe twice in their lifetime they have a tough and uncomfortable ride, but have you ever been in a New York or Tokyo subway at peak hours? Now that's tough—really packed—and commuters have to do it twice a day for the rest of their working lives.

When cattle reach the end of their productive life, it's instant. No lingering in pain, no loss of body functions, no agony or tube-feeding existence. There's no depression in anticipation of the end. Bang! It's over.

Isn't it better to have lived a good life, albeit short for some, than never to have lived at all?

YESTERDAY . . . WHEN I WAS YOUNG

When I was driving a tank in northern France and into southern Germany, I almost always drove with my seat extended up, the hatch open, and my head completely out of the vehicle. To drive it any other way was uncomfortable. The only times I remember driving with the hatch closed was in training or when we knew we might be under fire.

This was one of those button-down days. The Germans were known to line up their Tiger or Panther tanks in side streets of small towns to fire their 88 mm guns on our columns as we passed along the main street. Those shells could penetrate our Sherman tanks if they hit the right spot. However, when moving at twenty miles an hour—our top speed—it was difficult. We were much better off facing the enemy guns head on. We felt vulnerable from the side. They would use every trick in the book to make us stop so they'd have a stationary target. The orders from Patton's headquarters were to "keep moving—regardless."

This day, driving through a nameless town in Germany, I had the hatch closed and only the periscope for vision when I saw something in front of us. Out in the middle of our street was a temporary corral full of dairy cows. In the periscope they appeared to number a thousand, but I knew what I had to do—full speed ahead and no stopping. There are five men in a tank and we were all buttoned in and couldn't yell. Our excuse for a horn didn't do much. With my love of animals it was one of the toughest things I ever had to do. I have no idea how many were injured or killed but most of them broke out of the corral after hearing the bellows of the injured. To this day I don't know if there was an 88 cannon aimed at us from down that side street.

There were animals in front of me and men behind me. I ask all animal rightists of the world: What would you have done?

CHAPTER 10

ALL CREATURES ARE NOT CREATED EQUAL

It all started about 11:00 a.m. one Sunday morning. I glanced up at the sky and saw this huge black cloud moving toward us. It had a bright red glow at the base and lightning flashing throughout the dark mass. I had never seen a sky like that, and I thought, could this be Armageddon or just the storm to end all storms?

We were artificially inseminating our cows. We wouldn't normally work on Sunday, but when the cows are ready, you have to do it. You bring them into heat by injection so they're all ready at the same time. We were using semen from a very famous and therefore expensive bull, so we had no choice but to keep going. As the cloud moved closer, the cows grew more restless and harder to handle. Maybe it was the wrath of God for working on Sunday. All kind of thoughts were going through my mind. Gray flakes started falling like snow. What in the hell was this stuff? Then I did a dumb thing. I looked up and, of course, got some of this junk in my eyes. It hurt like hell.

Then it struck me. I'd been reading about the rumblings of Mount St. Helens, the volcano way over the mountains in southern Washington State. Could this be it? It had to be. It didn't seem logical in my mind because St. Helens was over one hundred miles away, but what else could it be?

We hurriedly finished working the cows as their backs were turning gray with falling ash and the sky was getting darker and darker. We went inside the house, just in time. By now it was totally black outside—blacker than the hole of Calcutta! We couldn't see the posts on the front porch. The birds had stopped singing and everything was perfectly still. It was midnight at high noon.

My wife and I sat and stared at each other and wondered how we would ever survive this disaster. Would the pastures go dead under the layer of ash? What would the cattle and other livestock eat? Would they survive inhaling this awful stuff? How dangerous was it? What about our cars and ranch equipment? We were pinned to the radio and television and tried to call family and the authorities, but all circuits were busy. If it was hitting us this hard a hundred miles away, what was it like in the rest of the state? How bad was the devastation? We needed to know.

It started to clear that afternoon about 3:00 p.m. I had a really sick feeling in the pit of my stomach. As it got brighter we peered out at a totally gray landscape. We slowly made our way outside and were shocked at what we found. It was difficult to believe that our ranch would ever be normal again.

As it turned out, we were on the outer edge of the worst hit areas. We were fortunate. We used a lot of circle irrigation and big traveling guns that sprayed water on the crops from above, so the ash washed off easily, unlike areas that use flood irrigation at ground level. The prevailing winds carried the ash all the way into Idaho and Montana and eventually around the world, but the brunt of it missed major metropolitan areas. About the worst we suffered was the immediate clean-up and an ongoing purchase of lots of filters for the equipment. The ash contained about sixty-four percent silica which is the basic ingredient of glass, plus traces of alumina, calcium, iron, silver, and gold. Under the microscope the ashes look like jagged pieces of glass shard which proved to be hard on engines. As to the effect in the long run, it seemed to be beneficial to the land, but those cows we'd artificially bred that horrendous day the mountain blew produced few calves. We had looked forward to

The day the mountain blew as the cloud moved over us.
The light sky behind the barn is red.

the results of our new breeding program, but the calves we did get weren't enough to validate our efforts. You can still see the ash along the Interstate 90 in the Moses Lake area. It was an experience I don't ever want to go through again.

As for our breeding program, we got going again, but like other ranchers, the cattle we sent to market weren't the same type as twenty years ago, nor are the steaks and roasts in the display cases. A lot of good things have happened to the cattle-breeding and livestock-feeding industries in the last twenty years. To satisfy and adapt to the new trends, the industry is sending younger and leaner beef to market—like twenty percent leaner. This may be a progressive move for cattlemen, but the problem I have with the whole program is that the pendulum has swung a little too far. Some beef has become too lean. The taste is gone and you need damned good teeth to chew it.

Too many of the livestock producers have gone into cross-breeding with exotic cattle to get heavier weights and longer legs. Those hump-backed, Brahma-based cattle shown in the photo on the next page are coming onto the market. They have the great ability to adapt to the kind of harsh climates found in the desert areas of our Southwest or in the lower elevations of countries near the equator. These cattle, originally from India, can survive tough and they taste tough. There is a place for these cattle and it's the rodeo circuit—not in a steak house, nor on your dinner table, nor in my North Forty. Even some of the best breeds are headed in the wrong direction by the registered breeder. Angus and Herefords, and the resulting crossing of these two excellent breeds (black baldies), should not be bred for quantity (size) at the expense of quality. I believe integrity of selection will eventually force pure-bred breeders back to reality.

I think breeders should be required to visit the packing houses and check the primal cuts from their animals before they're fabricated. A huge carcass does not make for the right-sized porterhouse or T-bone steaks, or for that matter some of the other retail

Black Angus in a pastoral setting

Brahma cattle

cuts. Who wants a steak half an inch thick? The direction should be back to the English breeds—the Angus, the Herefords, the Short Horns, and the like.

So that you can talk to your butcher intelligently, I'll give you more information than you'll ever want to know about beef. I also want you to become more aware of the cattle in those pastures as you drive by the countryside, or more important, as you walk through those fields. I'm sure you'll keep an eye on the bulls, but with the English breeds it's the cows you have to watch, especially the ones with calves. Don't take your dog into a pasture full of cows. The mamas will pay no attention to you but will go for the dog—and you know where that pet's going to run to be protected, so take care. I speak from experience!

It never bothered me to have a picnic by the river near English cattle. With all my years around Angus, I've never been bothered by a bull or cow, but I can't say the same for the exotic breeds. They are harder to move and have been known to go after a horse you're riding. They're also great fence jumpers. Those reasons alone account for the meat being tougher. One more word of advice: Don't ever go in a pasture with a dairy bull you don't know—go the other way, fast. You need not fear the dairy cows; they're generally pussycats. Actually, I don't recommend that anyone should approach an animal they don't know or even walk through a pasture uninvited.

Before I get off the subject of bulls, there is one other thing you might notice when driving by the cattle range—a single bull on a fence line totally ignoring his cows at the other end of the pasture. He's probably plotting to cheat a little on his girls. I've run across a worse scenario. I bought a beautiful five thousand dollar bull at an auction with registration papers up the ying-yang, brought him home, put him in the pasture with the "girls" and found out he preferred an alternative lifestyle. He seemed to be forever hanging out on the fence line, checking out the other bulls. Sometimes you can take an animal like that back and other times you're not so lucky. You also could collect his semen by artificial means, then impregnate the cows—but that takes a lot of time and money. A cow or two or three might have the alternative lifestyle, but not to worry, they're going to get "nailed" regardless. There's no such thing as just saying NO.

On the Black Angus Ranch two railroads went through the property and both created different problems in the raising of cattle. Basically, they killed them on impact. Also, the railroad caused panic in the herds the first few days the animals were put into an adjoining pasture. But I've always had a fascination with trains, and despite the tragedies, I never got tired of watching them travel through the property. Once in a while, I'd get an extra treat when they both would go through at the same time—whistles blowing.

If I heard a steady whistle, day or night, I knew some animal was on the track. If it didn't get out of the way fast enough, it meant trying to get reimbursed for the lost animal. The history of responsibility is well known. In theory, for the right of passage through your property, a railroad must maintain the extensive fencing and is considered negligent in the case of invasion by an animal. In practice, the Milwaukee Railroad paid the agreed-upon value of the livestock, but in their own sweet time. On the other hand, the Empire Builder or Great Northern Railroad never paid. They took the attitude, "So? Sue us," knowing damn well it would hardly be worth it. The only practical solution was for us to maintain the fences.

The railroad not only bothered the cattle, they gave all of us at the ranch, workers and visitors alike, plenty of opportunity to live on the edge. At one spot on the ranch, a railroad bridge crossed the Yakima River. We loved to dive off the trestle into the cold river, especially on a hot day, but we damned well had to keep an ear cocked for the sound of a locomotive approaching. It was strictly against the rules of the road, but what were they going to say to me? After all, they owed me for some registered cows they'd bumped off.

The real thrillers were the two tunnels that carried the Milwaukee Railroad under parts of the ranch. We found them to be great shortcuts between the south and north forties. You could see the light at the end of the shorter tunnel as soon as you entered it which gave us hope. Knowing railroads, we couldn't count on schedules, nor could we count on sound because the engines were still electric. What we found worked best was to feel the vibration in the rails. At this point the train followed the twists and turns of the river bank. As the engine approached the tunnel, it was moving at a relatively slow speed. We had a chance but only if we hurried.

The longer tunnel was too much! For one thing, you couldn't see daylight. It was also full of snakes, dead deer, and sometimes cow carcasses. Eventually the railroad abandoned this tunnel, but even then we didn't move our cattle through it. Occasionally, we'd ride horses through it, and they didn't like it much either. There was a plus side: In the heat of a mid-summer's day, the tunnels were always cool, and they drew all kinds of critters—including us, the cowboys.

We did have one cow who jumped fences, just like a deer, and when I saw it I couldn't believe it. Many of the exotic breeds can do this, but rarely an Angus. She went anywhere she wanted, and it was bound to happen—she got whacked by a locomotive. It's always a sad day to bury one of your mother cows.

Believe it or not, these animals have different personalities. If you've ever had the time to observe cattle in a pasture over a period of time, you'd notice they have many of the same traits as we have. There's a boss cow and there are submissive cows. Some are silly and some are so laid-back they even saunter through the dreaded cattle squeeze. This is a contraption you use when you're working the cattle such as tagging them. It gently constrains the animal so it can't move around, and it clanks and rattles as you open and close it. There are good mothers and others who don't give a damn. There are the over-sexed cows and those with frequent "headaches" who don't much care whether or not they get boinked by the bull.

Sometimes you'll notice a bunch of calves lying down and in the middle stands one cow. She's the baby-sitter. But should a coyote or dog enter the field, watch those mothers come running. Cows usually graze within sight of each other and in groups. If one lies down, so do a lot of others, and in bad weather they'll huddle together to share some body heat for protection from the storm. You've heard the term "contented cows." That comes from chewing their cud. They have four stomachs and they regurgitate their food and chew it finer. Sort of like carrying a picnic basket. I don't know of any fellow rancher who doesn't know his animals individually and become somewhat attached to them. The average herd in this country is thirty-five head, and many cattlemen even name each cow.

The offspring of these herds go into feed lots where corn or other grains are fed to them for a short time. These lots use screenings or waste from our grain production—corn and potato waste (phew), apple pumice, sugar beet sludge, and many other such leavings. What do you suppose would happen to all this waste if we couldn't feed it to animals whose stomachs are designed to digest it? We'd have a major disposal problem ("Oh, but please, not in my backyard!") if it weren't converted to edible protein by cattle.

We used horses to move cattle herds but not as much as in earlier years. Instead of saddling up every day, we jumped on the new four wheel Honda ATVs, screwed the big irrigation guns on the back, and drove through special cattle guards designed to allow us in but keep the cattle out. This way we could drive from field to field without having to open gates. When we wanted our cattle on fresh pasture, we had them trained so well, all we had to do was open the gate to that area, ring a bell and get out of the way. If there were an easier way to do it, I'd find it.

When friends would come over from the city, they loved to hop on a horse and play cowboy. This drove the cows and calves nuts, caused stress, and toughened their meat. We just used old dogs and Hondas. Of course, nothing works like a good quarterhorse when it comes to moving a herd up to the mountain pastures or rounding them up in the fall to get them back to the lower elevations for winter. It behooves all of us cattlemen to treat our herds with TLC. They sustain us in a way of life that will become a thing of the past if we do otherwise. Compassion and profit go hand in hand.

The following are some terms you should know:

Aged Meat: Dry aging is choice or prime beef hung for three or four weeks in a temperature-controlled room or locker. In this time the muscle fibers break down resulting in firmer, more tender, and more flavorful beef. Wet aging refers to storage at refrigerated temperatures in a vacuum package bag. Both methods have the same effect in tenderizing the meat.

Brine: Salted water used to preserve meat. Spices and herbs can be added to improve flavor. The meat is usually soaked in this solution for two weeks.

Bull: An uncastrated male beef animal. Bull meat is sometimes available and can be a good buy. If young enough, it can be very lean and have great flavor. See Chapter 13 for more on this.

Chicken-Fried Steak: Boneless beef sliced thin, coated with bread crumbs, and fried. Leaner cuts can be pounded first to tenderize them.

Cow: A mature female beef animal having given birth to one or more calves. The meat from this animal is sold only as commercial beef and generally used for ground beef.

Forequarters: The front half of the beef carcass is split lengthwise into two forequarters. Each half contains the brisket, chuck, rib, and plate sections. (See chart on pages 176 and 177.)

Hanging or Dressed Weight: This is the weight of the carcass before trimming.

Heifer: A female beef animal that has never had a calf. There are a great number of heifers that come into the market but sex of an animal is not put on labels. They make excellent tasting beef.

The better ones are used for replacements in a cow herd or sold to other breeders.

Hindquarter: The back half of the carcass. This quarter contains the short loin, flank, sirloin, and round sections. (See chart on pages 176 and 177.)

Kosher Meat: Meat that has been slaughtered, inspected, and approved according to rabbinical law of the Jewish religion.

Muscle-boning: Dividing muscles at the natural seams and making them into boneless cuts.

Primal Cuts: Any one of the cuts a side of beef may be divided into before being wholesaled.

Proten Beef: Proten is a trademarked name for tenderizing beef by using a derivative of papaya.

Saltpeter: A potassium-nitrate compound used to preserve meat.

Steer: A young, castrated, male beef animal from which a large percentage of our beef is derived.

Tenderize: To break down the less tender meat fibers by pounding with a special mallet, scoring with a knife, grinding, soaking in marinade, aging, or jecarding. The latter involves using closely aligned, needle-like prongs that puncture the meat and break down the tissue.

Veal: Young beef animal of either sex which is selectively fed and slaughtered at approximately three months.

You now know more about cattle raising than you probably really care to, but you're also informed enough to discuss it with your butcher. That's important, because he'll respect you more and give you the better cuts.

BEAUTY OF THE BEAST

An old slogan came out of the packing houses that said, "Everything from the animal is used except the moo." Very few people really know what a cow provides.

After beef protein, the most well-known product that comes from cattle is leather. From the time the first loincloth was donned in prehistoric times to the days of the Harley-Davidson, leather has added so much to the days of our lives. It's now a nine-billion-dollar-per-year industry.

Cattle byproducts add so much more to our everyday living that the consumer is generally unaware of. First, starting with the edible, did you know that the gelatins in products such as ice cream (Oh, boy!), yogurt, marshmallows, and mayonnaise all come from the bones of the cow? Another is the fatty acid-base in oleo margarine and shortening, and even chewing gum. The plasma protein is used in cake mixes, pasta, and imitation seafood.

Now, stay with me on this—it gets better. Man and cow have practically been joined at the hip through the centuries. We take care of them and they take care of us in so many different ways. They're a walking pharmacy. For instance:

FROM THE PANCREAS:
Insulin for the diabetic
Glucagon to treat hypoglycemia
Pancreatin to aid digestion
Trypsin and Chymotrypsin to promote healing for burns and wounds

FROM THE BLOOD:
Blood plasma: Fraction 1 - for hemophilia
Fraction V - kills viruses
Albumin - for R.H. factor types
Thrombin - blood coagulant
Iron - for anemia

FROM THE BONE:
Bone marrow - for blood disorders
Soft cartilage - used in plastic surgery
Bone meal - calcium and phosphorous source

FROM THE INTESTINES:
Medical sutures

FROM THE PITUITARY GLAND:
Pressor hormone - regulates blood pressure
ACTH - in drugs for arthritis and allergies

FROM THE SPINAL CORD:
Cholesterol for hormone products

Knocks your socks off, doesn't it? And there's more to come.

We are surrounded daily by products from this renewable resource—our cows: the soap you wash your face with, the baseball equipment in your closet, the artist painting with a cow-hair brush, the film in your camera, everyday chemicals and textiles, and commodities adapted for our health care. How about all those harnesses and saddles people use with their horses?

If we were to lose our cattle, the butcher, baker, and candlestick maker all would be in trouble. So would businesses that produce pharmaceuticals, chemicals, and textiles. Are you aware that the meat industry is the second largest manufacturing and processing industry in the nation? Whenever I hear something is second, I want to know who or what was first. So, in this case, I'll tell you. The automobile industry is first. Ranching/farming is also the second most dangerous occupation in the nation. What's first? Well, not mining, as you might think—that's third. The ironworkers who build our high-rise buildings are number one. Correspondingly, these occupations have the highest workmen's compensation insurance premiums to pay the state, another burden for the rancher.

When you think about it, the beef industry is more of an active part of our economy than you probably ever realized. Did you know that the byproducts from cattle help us get where we're going?

Thinking about the going, I logged thousands and thousands of miles in covering our areas of restaurant expansion. One early evening, I was going to Dallas from Los Angeles with one of the suits from Saga named Rich Quistgard. A flight delay gave us an opportunity to grab a couple of martinis in Delta's lounge before boarding, which put us in a mellow mood. As we boarded and sat down in our first-class leather seats, we were in good humor, laughing and enjoying ourselves. As soon as we were in the air and the seat-belt sign turned off, we buzzed our stewardess. "Nurse, we need medicine," we said—or something dumb like that. She looked at us and said, "Sirs, I believe you have mistaken me for someone who gives a shit!"

As she walked back down the aisle, we gasped and sobered up. What had she said? An airline stewardess yet?

A moment later, she marched back to where we were sitting, smiled and said, "I've been wanting to say that to a passenger for years; I took one look at you guys and just knew I could get away with it."

We broke up laughing. Wherever she is, flying or not, I hope she's still having that much fun.

Sorry, I digress, but certain things I write trigger old memories.

Back to the contribution of cattle to flight and other forms of transportation. The acids from inedible beef fats and protein are used for all sorts of lubricants. Antifreeze contains glycerol, a derivative of these acids, which keeps your car from freezing up. Your rubber tires hold their shape with stearic acid from our animals.

Cattle products are employed in airplane lubricants and runway foam. Car polishes and waxes are derived from these products, and when you drive or fly, don't forget the leather seats that are so comfortable and easily maintained. In olden days, cow dung was used for fire, so our ancestors could keep warm and cook. In modern days at the ranch, we used cow pies for some risky games of Frisbee.

No one has to use a product of a trade they don't believe in, and I can respect that. But if you're sincere, you need to think about all the endeavors in life you have to avoid. In the case of cattle, that means you can't eat meat or wear leather goods, and if you review the list above, you'll realize there's much more. You

can't travel in autos or planes, you'll have to be careful in supermarkets, and I hate to think about how restricted you'll be in a
hospital. If you are sincere in your efforts, stay home and don't
get sick. Check labels carefully before you paint your house or
wash your hands. Cattle products are used in bandages, wallpaper,
sheet rock, emery boards, and glues. If you need cosmetics, forget
about it.

I recently read where Bob Barker, the host of the *Price is Right*,
had a car removed as a prize for his show because it had leather
seats. That's correct—you read it right. Okay, Bob, you have the
right to your opinions and I respect that. If you really want to
make a statement, review all the above, and do it all the way.

Speaking of cosmetics, I can't get off the subject of the beauty
of the beast without mentioning what they do for our women and
some men. Collagen, the protein derived from the animals' skins
and hides, is utilized extensively in many cosmetics. It really
warms the heart when you hear of this product being used to dress
wounds and playing a part in repairing the skin of severely burned
individuals. It's employed in dentistry and in medicine to reduce
bleeding. It's best known use, however, is with the plastic surgeon
and the dermatologist.

In 1994 our hide exports were worth $1.4 billion, our export of
meat and animal fats amounted to $5.8 billion, and live animals were
worth almost six million, all of which help our balance of trade (which
sure can use all the help it can get). Over five billion pounds of
inedible tallow is exported each year and that's a bunch. (The above
figures are taken from a 1996 almanac.)

Why would we consider jeopardizing the employment of
many, giving up the world's most complete protein, and denying
people the joy of a great steak because of a small minority who
want to avoid meat and/or its byproducts for whatever reason.
Why let them put a guilt trip on those of us who love and appreciate the good qualities of meat? Statements condemning other

people's choices should not be tolerated when it does no harm to our environment (covered in Chapter 9) or to each other.

Speaking of harming the environment, vegetarian meals need rice, beans, and other grains for their protein. Large amounts of water are needed to grow these crops. Many of them can grow only in certain areas, have to be harvested by diesel equipment, and must be shipped many miles by trucks—both of which pollute the air. Nitrogen-rich fertilizer has been poured on these crops, and it's still unknown what this might be doing to our aquifers. Extreme activists won't wear leather—which is renewable and bio-degradable—so what takes its place? It's usually a synthetic or plastic material that often involves mining, pollutes the air and ground in its manufacturing, and is not always biodegradable.

All I'm saying here is, don't be too quick to judge others. We all have to share this earth, so working together to keep her healthy is the best answer. I'm sorry to say there are some people out there using this "environmentalism" business to get rich, and scare tactics help them succeed. It's important to remember that things are not always what they seem. Get all the facts so you can make truly informed decisions.

You now have some idea of what a beautiful role that beast plays in our lives. Consider all these benefits before condemning the use of byproducts from these great animals who roam the land. Most important, I can't emphasize enough that cattle industry products are renewable resources. I know I've written about this re-newable stuff before, but I find a need to repeat it. The packing houses are the original recyclers, using everything except the moo. Actually, the moo was recorded for one of our radio ads—soooooo?

CHAPTER 11

YOU MAKE
THE CALL

Have you ever felt like you needed to do something stupid? The urge is there—it's your time. What do you do? You go to an auction! Any auction. What it sells doesn't matter and you're sure to satisfy that itch.

With me it was either cattle, horses, Western art, or farm equipment, and I usually came home with something I didn't need, had paid too much for, and later wished I could take back. This is better known as buyer's remorse. People like me are usually easy to spot—we're enthusiastic and frequent bidders and the auctioneers are always tickled to see us arrive.

Jack Parnell, the premier Black Angus cattle auctioneer (see photo on page 144), became a good friend and we and our wives had some great visits together. Jack owned a ranch out of Auburn, California, with a herd of registered Black Angus cattle and Clydesdale draft horses, a restaurant called "The Headquarters," a meat market, and a nine-hole golf course. Along with these and his career as an auctioneer, he also became prominent in California and national politics. I always felt Jack should get a life and do something with it.

Even though we were good friends, he wasn't above getting more bids out of me. He knew I was a big boy and a businessman, so his friendship wouldn't slow him down from getting every dollar he could for that animal in the ring. After all, he was representing the seller.

Jack Parnell and me

Feeders and replacement cattle are generally sold at auction, but those sales are of pens or groups of cattle generally equal in size and age. These auctions are held frequently at local sales yards. That isn't the kind of auction I'm talking about here. I'm referring to the purebred market where the highly bred cows and bulls are sold individually in the ring. Most breeders hold an annual sale of registered animals which can be traced back through many generations by their papers. The Black Angus Association also holds shows with judging preceding the sale. The judging today tends to select the leaner animals. Of course, the winners usually bring the biggest money.

Here's where you can bid up to $10,000, $50,000, and $100,000 or more per animal. Because of the high costs involved, two, three, or more individuals or ranches will often combine to purchase one outstanding bull. I believe the record for an individual Black Angus bull was $750,000. A bull can breed naturally, alternating between ranches, but the general practice is to sell semen from the highest-priced bulls. Used naturally, the prized bull will service twenty-five or so registered cows and must be kept in a separate pasture so you can be positive which bull is the sire when it's time to register the offspring.

I like that word "serviced." There was a pill that came out allowing a bull to service more than one hundred cows instead of the normal twenty-five. I don't know what was in that pill, but I'll tell you this, it sure tasted bitter!

It was logical for me, raising so many Black Angus cattle, to eventually get into the registered Angus business, which is an entirely different ball game. Here you try to breed for perfection to increase the value of your breeding stock. It's a business that takes a great deal of bookkeeping and care in the field; you need to know exactly when which bull was in what field with whom. The papers must honestly reflect purity of bloodlines. To keep the breed pure, blood testing has been done on a regular basis in recent years.

There are fourteen years between these two pictures. Note the difference in height and size, and how market animals have changed.

Like so many businesses, this one, too, has its dark side. New, inexperienced breeders are sometimes fleeced by the principal actors in the charade that's part of the promotional side. Some of these guys would make used-car salesmen look like angels. I had the unfortunate experience of operating with more than one of these characters during my first few transactions.

In the Black Angus Ranch's attempt to raise leaner beef for the restaurants and markets, my wife and I attended many a registered Black Angus cattle auction. We visited most major livestock shows with cattle judging. These events were good places to meet and spend time with fellow breeders, and we were always on the look-out for special breeding stock sold at the auctions or by private treaty. From the late sixties to the early eighties there were dramatic changes in what became desirable (see photos on the left). The desire to go from waist-high cattle to almost head-high in less than twenty years was bound to create some dangerous practices by the charlatans in the business. I remember one of the judges at a big show was feeling the muscling on an Angus and his hand came away black. What was going on? There was a white spot on the bull's hide and it had been stained black. That whiteness in the wrong spot was a dead giveaway that the animal had Holstein blood mixed in somewhere along the line. It was a pure-ass fake. Take care, it can happen at any type of auction. The good news is that the vast majority of breeders are of the highest integrity. It's the Slick Willies who take advantage of and abuse the trade.

Back to the business of auctions. I'm sure most readers won't be attending a cattle or even an art auction, but my experience, from hard-knocks bidding, would apply to any number of auctions the reader could or would attend, such as:

IRS: They conduct their own auction on boats, cars, household items, jewelry, etc.

U.S. Postal Service: You can bid on bins containing small appliances, radios, CDs, undelivered packages, and so forth.

City & State Governments: Police and state purchasing departments auction everything from bikes to real estate.

Defense Department: Holds auctions at military bases as often as every month.

The first thing I learned, and learned the hard way, was to always give myself plenty of time to examine the merchandise, whether cattle, cars, or whatever. I try to allow a few hours or preferably a day before the scheduled auction. Secondly, I determine the value of the product and decide what I'd be willing to pay and no more, then I stick with that price NO MATTER WHAT. I know it's easier said than done. There's a kind of feeding frenzy that can start—it's like the sharks that smell blood in the water. Often I've seen prices start to escalate and go on past all reason—I've been there, done that. Sure, you can do something stupid, but you can also find a smart purchase at these auctions.

Some more tips: You might get a great buy on a cow at an Arizona auction, but how do you get her to your ranch in Eastern Washington? If an object you buy is going to be too big for your mode of transportation, you'd better find out how much it's going to cost you to get it where you want it—in advance.

What's it worth? You might be able to find out in a newspaper's classified section. Check the form of payment required as some might demand cash or a certified check. Bring a friend to a car auction—bet you can figure out why. If you make a mistake, like bidding on the wrong item—or worse, waving to your cousin across the way, a move that could result in the auctioneer pointing at you and saying, "Sold!"—correct it immediately, even if you're embarrassed. Shout it out if you have to. Saves getting stuck.

You want to drive auctioneer Jack crazy and maybe end up with a bargain? If he wants to start the item, whatever it may be, at a thousand dollars, shout out one hundred. Suppose the item's worth approximately five hundred dollars—you might get it for a hundred and fifty. Some auctions you can cut the tension with a knife but

The crowd at one of our Western Experience Sales—notice how every-one is practically sitting on their hands. This is a smart thing to do if you're not buying the piece on the auction block.

I'm enjoying the price brought by one of our sale heifers with friend, Grazzi Dano, and my wife, Helen.

nothing happens and there are no bids. You might be able to find the owner and negotiate—depending on the rules of that particular auction. I've seen a bidder bid against himself. Sounds dumb, but you'd be surprised how often that happens. Any class auctioneer like Jack will not allow that to happen.

A few years back I ran across a cowboy artist by the name of Fred Oldfield. I don't quite remember who promoted whom, but the association between us became mutually beneficial. Fred knew every cowboy whoever even thought of picking up a brush and palette. He's a very charismatic guy and you're aware of him as soon as he enters a room. He knows the best and the brightest in the Western art world and he had an idea how we could put our two connections together—and so the "Western Experience Sale" was born in the fall of 1980.

We held this auction function at the big party barn on the ranch. It was a two-and-a-half-day event where we sold highly valued, registered cattle and Western art (some prefer the term American art) alternately. The registered cows came from all over the West, as did the distinguished artists who brought their very best for sale.

We'd sell a cow that was paraded around the stage by a groom. Then we'd auction off a piece of art shown by a pretty woman. Food and booze were constantly available and the ninety-dollar-per-person admission fee was well worth the "experience." The event included seminars, dancing, quick draws (people watching as artists produced the work they'd later sell at auction), hot-air balloon rides, and tours of the ranch in a hay wagon pulled by our Clydesdale hitch. There was one gentleman who sold some of his cattle in our sale, Mac Cropsey, who was from Ankony Shadow Isle Ranch in Colorado. This operation was owned by the late oil mogul Armand Hammer. Cropsey didn't pay his commission on his cattle we sold, which represented the difference between profit and loss that year. It was that close. But we all had a lot of fun and that's worth a lot. We did make about six thousand dollars the following year, but that didn't include personal labor. We really

Getting ready for and enjoying the Western Experience sale

Fred Oldfield in his office at our barn

couldn't have done what we did without the help of our secretary, Kris Thorpe, who fell in love with the art world and is still at it in Scottsdale, Arizona. We decided it was way too costly timewise and stopped doing it after three years. We have regrets about that because the artists loved it and we loved them and have maintained contact with many of them. It's been fun to watch their work improve as years go by and the prices climb accordingly.

Although cattle auctions generally didn't include alcohol, art auctions did—to the detriment of some bidders, including me one time. This big boo-boo taught me to pay attention.

Jack Parnell was the auctioneer this particular evening and he and his floor men knew I had a devious way of bidding. After a cow from California sold big, setting the mood for the day's proceedings, a large watercolor painting by Joe Bohler came on the block. It depicted two draft horses pulling a feeding sled through the deep winter snow on a ranch that partly resembled an area of mine, and I fell for it hard.

I wasn't born blind on this one. I had examined it well in advance, as all good bidders are supposed to do, and because of the artist, I knew it would be a good investment. I started my bid ridiculously low, as all good bidders do, and wrote down my top price which I would stick to, as all good bidders should.

Then I used a method of bidding that I'd perfected over the years at auctions. With an auctioneer who knew me, such as Jack, I could submit a bid even without the person sitting next to me knowing. This was done with little sneaky signals. I could stay in the action unnoticed. As the price increased I searched for my competitor; I could feel it was only one person by the way the floor men were acting. But it's a huge barn and the crowd was big. I had no luck. I knew I was being pushed and ended up going over my limit—as usual.

After passing this figure by more than I'd like to admit, I bought the painting only to find out that all along I'd been bidding against my mother. The floor men didn't know my mother and

153

How could I blame my almost-ninety mother?

Painting by Joe Bohler now hanging in my bathroom-to-end-all-bathrooms.

HIGH COUNTRY WINTER   **28"x 30"**

were unaware of this in-house dual. She was trying to buy the painting for me for Christmas and my birthday combined. She was watching me, knowing I had expressed a love for the painting, but she didn't see me bidding so kept on going. Not very s-m-a-r-t! I was torked off and now I know where that saying—"Quit blaming your mother"—comes from.

• • • • • • • • • • • • • •

Now for the biggest and scariest auction experience of my life. When Saga finally died, it was evident that the Black Angus Cattle Company would no longer be used for television commercials, charity functions, or company business meetings, so I had to rethink my future.

In one of my visits with Ernie Arbuckle, the chairman of Saga's board, he talked about changing his job recently and used the expression, "It was time to re-pot myself." That's where I was right now, but it could take years to sell a ranch this size during a fragile economy with high interest rates. It had taken me a long, long time to build it up and improve it—not just the increased acreage but the addition of sophisticated irrigation systems, improved efficiency, and such beautification as miles of white fencing. I wanted to end the pain quickly, and I've never been a patient man. I decided to divide the ranch into five separate ranches, each capable of operating on its own, and auction all of them off, one by one. This would be followed by the sale of the cattle, horses, sheep, and finally the equipment, all at separate auctions.

These auctions—particularly the land sale—created one of the more intense times of my life, right up there near the front-line action of the war and the merger of my business with Saga Corporation. Childbirth, marriages, and divorces also rank in there somewhere.

We hired one of the largest real estate auction companies in the West, Kennedy-Wilson, to promote the event with ads in *The Wall Street Journal*, livestock and ranch publications, local newspapers, and so forth, and to produce and mail out beautiful color brochures.

THE REAL ESTATE CORNER

FARMS / RANCHES / ACREAGE

WASHINGTON   WASHINGTON

REAL ESTATE AUCTION

Stuart Anderson's
Black Angus/ Cattle Company Ranch

Stuart Anderson's internationally famous Black Angus/Cattle Company Ranch is located in central Washington in the fertile Kittitas Valley (which averages more than 320 days of sunshine) beside the beautiful Yakima River in the foothills of the Cascade Mountains. Easy freeway access provides breathtaking views of the surrounding Wilderness Areas and National Forests. The ranch fronts US 90, and is 40 miles north of Yakima and 98 miles east of Seattle.

The ranch (no longer used for the marketing of the Black Angus/Cattle Company Restaurant chain) is offered in 5 parcels totaling some 2,500+ acres, of which 1,620 acres ± is under irrigation. Parcels include homes, barns, silos etc. Parcel 5 is improved with a spectacular 6,000 square foot home, large entertainment facility, tennis court, volleyball courts and baseball diamonds.

For Auction Brochure call (800) 237-6517.

BROKER COOPERATION

KENNEDY-WILSON, NORTHWEST
510 SW THIRD AVENUE, SUITE 200
PORTLAND, OREGON 97204

Ad as it appeared in *The Wall Street Journal*

All this promotion created an influx of different types of people from around the world. I had not renewed the lease on the range land so all the land to be sold was deeded and now comprised just over twenty-six hundred acres. With that much territory, it took me a long time to show all the different visitors the now five separate ranches—even wined and dined several of them. We spent day after day with everyone from serious buyers to "Lookie Lou's." I especially felt the latter applied to three gentlemen from Taiwan. (One thing Asians should never do is wear big cowboy hats. It just doesn't look right.) How wrong I was about these Taiwanese—it was a rush to judgment on my part. I didn't realize it at the time, but these gentlemen were looking for a site for a golf course resort.

We had to make arrangements for housing, food, and travel for the auctioneers, floor men, and out-of-state participants. The whole package cost more than $125,000—quite a gamble, not knowing whether we'd get any action or not. I had high anxiety.

The day came and started slow. There were less than half the people who attended our Western Experience Sale, and I didn't know if any of them were serious buyers. I'm generally laid-back and often appear bored, but this day I couldn't sit still. Even though newspaper reporters were flown in by private planes and helicopters, I wouldn't give them an interview.

Then it began. The first parcel, an eight-hundred-acre ranch with river frontage, house, two barns and corrals, was started by the auctioneer at the minimum of $465,000. It drew zero bids. Zippo! Nothing! Then came Parcel No. 2 which was the upper ranch with three big circles on good pasture with miles of fencing and two ponds. (This was the only parcel without houses or out-buildings.) It would fit naturally with any of the parcels. Same result—no bids. Then Parcel No. 3 was put on the block. This one had freeway exposure, a full setup of buildings with two silos, two homes, a shop, an automated feed lot and some of the best cropland on the entire ranch. It also included an efficient irrigation system. Again—no bids! I was getting more traumatized by the

Parcel Number 4

minute. I had to get out of the barn which resulted in the picture below on the front page of the *Seattle Post-Intelligencer*. One of my more flattering pictures, it told the story.

For the sake of my business, I've always sought publicity and managed to get a lot of pictures in the paper, but never on the front page of a Seattle newspaper.

I could still hear the auctioneer as he was starting on Parcel No. 4. I felt like shouting, "Wake up, there are real bargains here! Does anyone have a pulse?" I almost screamed out a bid myself just to hear someone's voice besides the auctioneer's. But there was just silence from me and the crowd. Parcel No. 4 was the original ranch I had purchased. It had a new, double-wide, modular home, a single mobile home, our previous house which had been remodeled, a large stock barn with chutes, cattle squeezes, and the corrals needed to handle high numbers of cattle. The irrigation system was operated by gravity flow, so no electric power was needed to operate the three circles, wheel moves, and traveling sprinkler guns. The auctioneer tried all the normal ploys but nothing came of them. I was getting sicker by the minute.

It was stated in the sales brochure that Parcel Nos. 1, 2, 3, and 4 would be combined and auctioned at a ten percent increase of the minimum published bids for all four ranches. We were at that point where an attempt would be made to sell all four parcels together at ten percent over the minimum bids. Parcel No. 5, which comprised our home, the large sale or party barn, Yakima River and Taneum Creek property of some two hundred and fifty acres, had an unpublished minimum and it was to be auctioned after the first four were sold.

Then I heard it—a sound from the crowd. It was the most welcome voice in the world. One man had made a bid for all four ranches. Hard as the auctioneer tried to elicit more bids, nothing else was said. "SOLD!" What kind of auction was this? A single bid on four ranches at the minimum plus ten percent. Then our home ranch went on the auction block and received no bids which

GRANT HALLER/P-I

Stuart Anderson, center, listens to an auctioneer sell his 2,400-acre Black Angus cattle ranch near Ellensburg. With him yesterday were Bobbi Loughrin, left, Anderson's bookkeeper for 17 years, and Jay Gorman, a family friend. Anderson's house on the ranch was not sold.

Steak king sells cattle ranch for $1.7 million

By Ed Penhale
P-I Reporter

ELLENSBURG — Super steakman Stuart Anderson auctioned off his cattle ranch yesterday, but he will live on in the Kittitas Valley where his brand has been known for more than 20 years.

The founder of the Black Angus/Cattle Company restaurant chain got $1.7 million for the 2,400-acre ranch in a one-bid auction.

No one bid on the spectacular house where he and his wife, Helen, live atop a butte overlooking the Yakima River.

And that was a relief to Helen Anderson, who said before the auction that if she and her husband could sell the ranch land, they could keep the home that had an asking price of $1.4 million.

The sale marked the end of an era for Anderson, the soft-spoken businessman-cowboy who starred in television commercials promoting the ranch and the more than 100 restaurants that once carried his name.

Now the beef baron has been put out to pasture. The latest owner of the restaurant chain, American Restaurant Group Inc., did not renew Anderson's contract

See **ANDERSON**, Page A4

Ranch auction *P.I.* photo showing desperate moment with friends Bobbi Loughrin and Jay Gorman

was exactly the way we wanted it. We had deliberately put a high minimum on that parcel. Most people said I made out like a bandit getting that extra ten percent. I always figure it's better to be envied than pitied. Did they pay an unnecessary $170,000 or was it shrewd planning on their part? Regardless, it was over. All of a sudden the tension was broken. WOW—never again!

The bidding was done by a gentlemen named Benjamin Shih who was representing a three-way, Taiwanese partnership. I later learned they were all sitting around someplace like Oklahoma reading *The Wall Street Journal* and saw our ad. One of them suggested they all go together and buy a big ranch and build a destination golf resort, dude ranch, and conference center. They came, they saw, they bought. Ah, the ironies of life.

If you're wondering why there is no resort after all this time, it's the old story of partners falling out of favor with each other. It's really a shame because they had hired the best and were going full bore toward their goal. Their plans were beautiful. I don't remember exactly how many issues came up on the Environmental Impact Statement, but it was a very large number. So, besides the partners' disagreements with each other, the bureaucrats were going to make it difficult and this, too, influenced their decision not to proceed.

CHAPTER 12

WATER, WATER, EVERYWHERE, NOR ANY DROP TO IRRIGATE

Water is the blood of the continent. But what's this got to do with beef? Everything! Water gives us the ability to dramatically increase production of apples, sugar beets, potatoes, carrots, sweet corn, and other vegetables, the refuse from which is fed to cattle. Irrigation increases the availability and lowers the cost of hay and grain fed to market animals. The lack of water in farming would substantially increase food costs in America, and that certainly includes beef.

Oil was the liquid gold of the twentieth century—water is destined to be the liquid gold of the twenty-first century. We are running out of water in the high plain states and could be in the same situation soon in the arid western states. California raises more vegetables than the rest of the country combined, but not without heavy irrigation. The increased demand for water from population growth, golf courses, crop needs, lawns, fish, wildlife, and other uses may soon exceed our resources. The fastest-growing cities in the West—Las Vegas and Phoenix—are running out of water. Are we depleting a nonrenewable water supply in some areas? We are, and it's not a very pretty picture.

As of this writing in 1996, there is ample water for a change in the West from rain and winter's snowfall. I took a trip with my wife, Helen, to Montana in July and found the rivers overflowing, the lakes and reservoirs at their maximum. As a rancher whose water has been cut off too early too many times, this was a pleasure to see. What a contrast with the huge water shortages we had in the West three of the last five years!

How quickly we all—ranchers, farmers, and consumers alike— forget the dangerous drought caused by the exceptionally dry weather. The tension will come back as strong as ever with the next shortages—destined to occur again. Some growers will face financial ruin. The hard feelings over how water is allocated between farmers is enough to make the Hatfields and McCoys look like kissin' cousins. Most farmers operate on low profit margins, and when the water is shut off before the growing season is finished, it can mean the difference between success or failure for the year. Maybe they don't get that second or third cutting of their crop, and that's a big loss. Other than having the water supply cut off, their only option is to dig deep wells which can cost as much as a hundred thousand dollars. It's not like they have a lot of choices. They cannot revert to dry-land farming; they would only be able, at most, to produce one-fourth of our current production.

America is the most dammed country in the world, with the possible exception of China. All our dams have brought us many benefits: cheap power, flood control, and, lest we forget the one we're talking about, irrigation. Without dams, the agricultural largess produced in the West would be reduced by more than seventy-five percent. There are more dam sites that could be developed, but is that the answer? The big river systems—the Columbia, the Colorado, and the Sacramento—account for a vast majority of the crops raised.

Along with the substantial benefits of dams, a few drawbacks have developed that weren't totally understood back when these systems were built. Ancient fish migrations have been disrupted. Sediment moving down river has now been trapped by the dams. The lack of organic matter that has been trapped in basins behind the dams has deprived the river banks of this sediment downstream, resulting in erosion.

Circle irrigating the Black Angus Ranch in Eastern Washington.

The eleven dams on the Columbia River have wreaked havoc on the salmon run and have brought that king-of-the-fish-world to his fins. There is no disputing that we need to help the migrating fish. One way is to increase the stream flow. This diversion of water to increase the flow takes away from irrigators, and so the views of fishermen and farmers find conflict. I want to see both beef and salmon on our menus at reasonable prices. I have never been a prophet of gloom and doom, and I'm not going to start now. It's just that we need to adopt changes to our current system or our future water problems will become severe. I'm not just telling you how bad things are; I have some ideas, from years of experience, on what we could do. I guess you knew this was coming.

Okay! Okay! What do we do about it? Are there solutions? Yes!

Irrigation farming as practiced in the West uses up to eighty-five percent of available water, so this is the logical place of attack—sorry about that if you're into farming. "Attack" is a poor choice of words. How about the place to look for some major changes? I should make it clear that the cattlemen in the above photograph (the farming foursome on the golf course) do not necessarily agree with me on my suggestions for change in irrigation practices. I would also like to stress that all citizens need to do their part in conserving water. According to P.J. O'Rourke, seventy-five percent of the water we go through in our homes is used in the bathroom, so his retort is, "Thank God. Think of the mess it would make in the den!" If you ask the average person what his source of water is, he would probably point to his faucet. We, as a nation, are far too wasteful with this valuable resource!

More storage for the spring run-offs would be a big help; however, the government and environmentalists are reluctant to back this expenditure until the water-users show a sincere effort toward conservation.

There is no incentive for individual farmers or ranchers to efficiently use or conserve the water that is allocated to them. First, I propose that habits, rules, and wasteful methods be changed and brought into the twenty-first century. Irrigators fasten your seat belts—no more senior and junior water rights. We've outgrown this antiquated system for determining where our irrigation water goes. It's un-American—how long do we pay for the omissions and sins of our fathers? We should all operate out of the same starting gate.

How's that for a beginning? Ancient rules do not make for a good irrigator. I sure don't want to lose my fellow cattlemen with grandfather rights on this. They'll probably disagree, but we need strong incentive to achieve our goals, and that comes from our capitalistic system. We know our economic system operates on supply and demand, profit and loss. All farmers and ranchers should be allotted water according to need (class of soil and number of acres) and then allow our system to go to work. The water district in which I owned land is currently allocating four acre-feet of water per irrigated acre registered with the district. This is the equivalent of water standing four feet deep on each irrigated acre you own. Try to visualize how much that is, but remember, one has the entire season to use it. If an efficient water-user can operate through the season with just a little over three feet, he or she doesn't even get a "Hello, nice job!" There is zero incentive to use less than what has been allocated, so why try? We have got to apply the American system—you operate efficiently, you realize some profit, and the better you do it, the more profit you receive. That's the fuel that drives our economy, so let's put it to work.

First, lower overall allocation by ten percent which would increase flow for power and/or fish. Then there should be an auction twice a year for surplus water—you think I have an auction fixation? Let's say it's mid-August in a water-short year. The irrigators would assemble—and then watch economic factors play their part. Water will be preserved and irrigation systems will become extremely efficient. I had a ranch neighbor who flooded his fields and just let the water run off so he could continue getting his allocation. He figured, if you don't use it, you lose it. In drought

Rancher/hotel mogul the late Jim Bridge, Helen, premier cattle feeder Don Schaake, his wife Peg, cattleman/irrigation district chairman Laurin Mellergaard, and me at a tailgate party

Me supervising the ranch irrigation from our house-on-the-hill swimming pool with friend, Bob Robbins, at cocktail hour

years, a person raising pasture or hay with efficiency would conserve his water, knowing he could profit from this practice by selling his excess to an orchardist or intensive crop farmer who needs it. The law of supply and demand would come to the forefront.

This would be the incentive water-users need to become more efficient, and there are many ways to accomplish this. The best methods would be to install circles with drop tubes close to the crop, wheel lines, or drip irrigation—unfortunately these are also the most expensive. A lot of water is delivered to fields in open ditches which is very wasteful. Piping the water to fields prevents evaporation and seepage, and just lining the ditches with concrete saves a lot of water from draining away. Why should the irrigator spend money doing these things if there is no remuneration? The same applies to old-fashioned flood irrigating, which should be replaced with more efficient methods, but what's the incentive? Why change the system? Arriving at the incentive pay and the details involved get rather complicated. I believe this is neither the time nor the place, but the wasting of water in irrigation districts is an ongoing concern but it can be resolved.

All our fields on the lower ranch were too rocky to raise crops other than pasture grass and some hay. For the intensive production of beef, it pays to irrigate, and we found where the fields were level enough that the most efficient method of irrigation was through the circle equipment in use so much in the dry areas of the West. That's how all those beautiful round green patches you see while flying over a lot of our country got there. One problem with this method of irrigating was that the wheels of the sprinkler towers killed the calves that lay down in the wet tracks to stay cool. They wouldn't hear the silent, advancing towers that carried the pipe and sprinklers. We put bells on, but that didn't help much because they grew accustomed to the sound. We then built little cowcatchers, like the trains have, to push the young calves out of the way, and that almost solved the problem. In the end, we found it best not to irrigate when the young cattle were in the pasture.

When the equipment was shut off we had a new problem. Cattle used the sprinkler heads, which were dropped down from the tower to make them more efficient, as back scratchers, knocking them off. We then replaced the metal drop pipes with soft water hoses. That got 'em. Who likes a wimpy back scratcher?

I experimented with intensive grazing to increase the pounds of beef raised per acre—with restaurant consumption always in mind. The longer cattle can exist on pasture, the leaner the finished product will be. In countries where land is dear, farmers are expert at this. I used wheel lines and circles on productive but rocky ground not suitable for crops. By stocking the cattle heavily and using electric fencing to confine the animals to a smaller grazing area, the ranch became far more efficient. It was a very financially worthwhile venture. As an end result, I never used the amount of water allocated to the ranch, for which I received zero credit. I placed two electric lines of wire across the fields as a fence. By spacing the insulated posts far enough apart where necessary, the tires of the wheel lines or circles could actually go over the wire in between, keeping the cattle confined while still irrigating the field. They'd be forced to clean that pasture totally before we opened the gate to the other side of the circle or the next section of field. This was done on a rotation basis so the area they started in would be rich with pasture grass by the time they got back there. Using this method, I found I could get ten head of cattle per acre feed-lot ready instead of the usual ratio of three per irrigated acre. The cattle would learn to respect that small fence in a hurry. Periodically, one animal would cautiously approach and touch the wire while the rest of the group watched. When he jerked back and bellowed, they stayed away until the next tester's turn came up.

Here again, I must remind the reader that these cattle are converting pasture land that's unsuitable for any other crop to protein, the building blocks of our bodies. Modern mechanical irrigation is expensive but very efficient, and I believe it's the wave of the future to bring unproductive ground into our food chain.

To paraphrase a famous quote, "The fault lies not in our supplies, but in ourselves," and using our supply of water inefficiently! Did you know that water covers more than seventy percent of the surface of the world? Speaking of water . . .

YESTERDAY . . . WHEN I WAS YOUNG

After completing tank school in Georgia, our battalion was sent to Camp Shanks in New York. Preparing to ship out to Europe, we headed to the harbor to board the troop carrier. As usual, the Army did everything by the book—alphabetically with the A's loading first. I headed one deck down, then another, and another, down, down, until I was at the very bottom of the ship. Four bunks were stacked alongside the bulkhead, and I was assigned the bottom one. This set-up would make anyone nervous. For the first time in my life, I realized I had more than a touch of claustrophobia. We were going to go across the Atlantic, which I pictured full of German U-boats, one of which would sink us, and I'd never be able to get out of the ship. That night I was panicking, but I had to stay macho. I didn't know what to do. I was dead! And then something happened . . . .

That night, I didn't sleep a wink. In the "I swear it's true" category, the ship got stuck leaving the harbor and we were at a standstill. Another troop carrier was brought alongside—they were going to transfer us. We started reloading—this time in reverse order so the Z's ended up in the bottom. The new ship was a little smaller, and when it came to the A's, no room. The powers that be—I could kiss 'em—put me, and a few others, outside on the deck. As I lay there on my little cot, I felt the Bluebird of Happiness was watching over me. There has never been, nor will be again, a luxury cruise ship with such accommodations as this—and water, water, everywhere.

Sometimes, one gets more than one deserves.

When the debt load fell off my back in my merger with Saga, I felt like I was a lottery winner. If you win the lottery and live in

The main salon of the Groote Beer

Seattle, you buy a boat. Seattle is almost totally surrounded by water—Puget Sound and Lakes Washington and Union—and is the boating capital of the world. I searched locally first and couldn't find one big enough, so off I went to Newport Beach, California, another city claiming to be the boating capital of the world. I discovered an ex-Navy boat that had been converted and was every bit as big as John Wayne's. I made an appointment for a test run the next day. When I arrived that morning, the captain couldn't get it started, so he told his mate to take the dinghy and show me the canals of Balboa while he got someone to fix it. During that cruise, I spotted the Groote Beer docked in one of the back canals. It was love at first sight. I had the dinghy pilot take me to her and found the owner. After making a deal, I removed the "For Sale" sign and sent the dinghy and flustered mate away. I hope the captain didn't give his mate too much hell—it wasn't his fault. The Groote was magnificent!

Wherever I sailed that boat—San Diego, San Francisco, and smaller ports—here came the media. They loved the fact this botterjacht had been built by Dutch slave labor for Hermann Goering. I once asked a young cocktail waitress in San Diego if she knew who Goering was. She thought for a few seconds and said "That used-car salesman who comes in all the time from Escondito?" NOT! He was Hitler's second-in-command in charge of the notorious Luftwaffe, the German air force, during World War II. I liked the fact he gave me a bad time in Germany, and now I owned his fabled North Sea boat, which he never took delivery of, thanks to the passive resistance of the Dutch builders.

She created so much interest because of her uniqueness—leeboards and all—that I want to answer some of the questions frequently asked about her. She was built of black oak and teak with wonderful gilding and carvings everywhere. The main salon even had a fireplace with a Delft-tiled facing. Her deck was fifty-two and a half feet long, with a wide seventeen-foot beam—a motor-sailer with a sixty-eight-foot mast and over two thousand

Groote Beer Becomes New Training Vessel for Boy Scouts.

On Christmas Day Stuart met with representatives of the Exploring Division of the Boy Scouts of America on board the Groote Beer (pronounced Grew-ta Beer) at the Seattle Yacht Club to donate his famous boat to the Chief Seattle Council of the Explorer Scouts. Stuart has owned the historical Dutch-built botterjacht since 1973. Probably no vessel of her size has compiled a world wide history and renown to equal this 52-foot vessel. Commissioned in 1938 (but never sailed) by Air Marshal Hermann Goering, it was built by Dutch and Danish craftsman in Holland and named for the Big Dipper.

The Groote Beer is distinguished for her marble and Delft tile, woodburning fireplace and the profusion of elaborate handcarving in teak throughout the boat. Gracious accommodations include two roomy staterooms, plus quarters for crew and a fabulous main salon.

The Explorer Scouts plan to use the Groote Beer as a training vessel for their boating activities.

The Groote Beer under sail in Puget Sound

Stuart "The Captain"

Hand carved figure of the "Great Bear" adorns the stern.

A page about the Groote Beer from our in-house newspaper, *Stu Who's News*

square feet of working sail area. She was flat bottomed with two, solid-teak leeboards, one on each side, to stabilize her in rough water. Pictures do not do justice to this beauty

We had some wonderful times aboard that boat. She displaced thirty-eight tons and took over two blocks to stop once thrown into reverse, which made going through the Seattle locks a real trick. One of the previous owners raced her from San Diego to Hawaii and she came in second to last. The last-place boat had lost its mast.

I had the boat completely refurbished but found we weren't using it enough to justify the money I was pouring into her, so I approached Charlie at Saga with the suggestion they place it on permanent mounts next to the Stuart's at Shilshole restaurant (which they now owned) with a boarding ramp to it. They could rent it out for special dinners. But just the beauty of her would have been great for business and enhanced the restaurant. Once again, the bean-counter mentality couldn't visualize such a thing, and the answer was a resounding "No!" I ended up donating it to the Sea Scouts, knowing it would be well cared for.

Stuart's at Shilshole. The third floor was our penthouse. It was beautiful but we can vouch for the truth of the old adage, "Never live above a restaurant!"

SECTION III

BUYING BEEF

(AT THE SUPERMARKET)

CHAPTER 13

IF YOU CAN'T TELL A
RUMP FROM A STUMP

If you're not the meat buyer or grocery shopper, you could skip this chapter. You have my permission. After all, it's your time. But if you want to know why your meat isn't as good as it used to be, read on.

I've got news for you—there is beef out there in the market that's labeled *choice* that isn't *choice*. Who sez? I sez! Determining the grade is a judgment call and not at all scientific. Not all the people who make those decisions are terribly experienced. Some are—some aren't. Packers use both USDA (United States Department of Agriculture) inspectors and graders who are hired and trained by the government. The inspector's time (not including overtime) is paid for by the USDA and then billed to the packer. In the case of USDA graders, the packer "commits" for all or part of a grader's time and is billed by the USDA for this commitment. Not the greatest situation, is it?

"This beef is USDA inspected." Big deal! All meat, even dog meat, must be inspected at the state or federal level, depending on where the meat will be sold. You should know that grading is not the same as inspecting for health. Thankfully, health inspecting is becoming more scientific, but you can read the next chapter for more on that.

Displaying the grade of meat is not mandatory, so many stores don't put anything on the package. If that's confusing, it's meant to be, because it works to the advantage of the supermarkets. The only way to work around the system is to become your own grader. Scary? Naw. Complicated? Not really. It's quite easy once you give it a try. Let me explain a couple of things.

In the beef business, grading is done with sight, feel, and smell. Graders check the color, which should be bright, clear, and crimson; the texture, which should feel firm; the smell, which should be fresh; and the marbling, the small spider-like ribbons of fat running through the meat. They then run a metal roller down the side and record the grade by a slap—three for *prime*, two for *choice*, and one for *select*. The next person notes this and moves the carcass down the appropriate line for handling. Another stamp sets the yield of the carcass, which doesn't affect the retail buyer, so we won't get into that. Graders make these decisions at least a hundred times an hour, and sometimes up to as many as three hundred times.

Just a few years back, seventy percent of all beef was graded *choice*. With such a large amount of choice, it was further broken down by the professional meat buyers into high choice, mid-choice, and low choice. The Black Angus chain specified high choice and had to pay more for it, which was money well spent. The same applied to butchers buying for meat markets and grocery chains—some bought the better beef because that's what their clientele demanded and were willing to pay for. To you, the customer, it was all marked *choice*. Now that the grading names have shifted to include the grade *select,* the percent graded *choice* has also dropped. This shift doesn't make it any easier for making decisions at the meat counter. To complicate things further, it's rare, but some supermarkets are buying *no-roll* beef which is meat not graded by the USDA. (It called that because *no roller* is run down the carcass to grade it.) The quality of this beef can vary a great deal and the meat market puts their own name on it such as *butcher's select* to further confuse the issue. What all this boils down to is that the grading system today can't be totally relied upon and you have to become the grader.

So how do you apply all this knowledge to your shopping for meat? Seek out the same things inspectors do, then observe the contents of all those pretty packages lined up so neatly in the meat counter to impress you. Pass by any meat cuts showing a slightly yellow fat. That's usually a sign the animal's been fed too long on grass and the meat is probably tough. Avoid packages with a lot of blood showing. That means it's been there too long or has been frozen and thawed. If it has large pockets of fat or a lot of fat on the edges, it hasn't been properly trimmed, so it's not a good buy. If it's frozen, skip any packages with lots of ice crystals because the meat's probably been thawed and refrozen. Also, don't always buy according to shape. Chuck steak can be shaped to look like a porterhouse. You should be cautious in relying on names alone as they can vary from store to store and state to state. It used to be that Kansas people weren't too familiar with the Kansas City steak, or that a New Yorker wasn't accustomed to ordering a New York steak. Names for the various cuts can be very confusing. Here is a list used at the restaurant level when buying from the packer. They're not exactly mouthwatering to put on a menu or on retail cuts of meat.

Hock	Butt
Blade	Rump
Pin Bone	Clod
Pot	

For buying, the jargon is hard. For selling, it becomes softer. We much prefer these delightful names because they sort of roll off the tongue:

Prime	Filet
Delmonico	Porterhouse
Top	Teriyaki
New York	Chateaubriand
Beef Wellington	Tenderloin
Sirloin	London

The supermarket might use these and other confusing names:

Butcher's Select	House Choice
Gourmet's Choice	His & Her Steaks

Forget them. They're just merchandising gimmicks. Study the chart on pages184-185. It gives you a good understanding of the basic cuts of beef and where they come from. For those more concerned about fat and calories, consider the "skinniest six." These are the cuts that usually have the words "Loin" or "Round" in their names—sirloin, top loin, tenderloin, top round, eye of the round, and round tip. Remember, LOIN IS LEAN. Got it? These cuts are lower in calories, contain less fat (the same as skinned chicken), and generally are an excellent buy for the health-conscious.

It's extremely unusual, but sometimes you can find bull meat called bullock beef. In my quest for leaner beef, we experimented with this at the ranch. We didn't castrate some bulls, but left them intact and fed them fast so they'd go to market young, tender, and exceptionally lean. To keep them from fighting we raised them together as young animals. But boys will be boys, you know. We built a shed with a low roof so they couldn't ride each other. All this activity toughens the muscle areas which is the part we eat. This experiment didn't last long because the wholesale buyers discounted the animals dramatically when they were marketed. Incidentally, men from Argentina wouldn't eat meat from castrated animals for a long time because . . . well, because it's a *guy* thing. Now that's macho! Maybe that practice hasn't changed. I do know that the bullock meat, when fed right, makes for excellent lean beef. The markets generally will not carry a product graded *bull* because of the name connotation. Kind of like trying to get the public to buy tom turkeys.

When in doubt, ring the bell and get the butcher. In the changing winds of time, butchering is almost a lost art—but not quite. A good butcher is worth his weight in gold, so treat him right. He's well aware that some of the extra-lean cuts of beef graded *select* are priced about the same and are sometimes more costly than *choice* steaks. In the beef business we've had the grade *good* forever. We all knew this was very lean, generally tasteless, and inexpensive. It was seldom found in any supermarket and wasn't used by restaurants either. Beef graded *good* could be found in economy displays in some markets and does have its place in pet foods and some processed meat. The fairly new grade *select* ranks between *choice* and *good* grades. The terminology *select* should be interpreted as a little better than *good* and somewhat less than *choice*, no matter how smoothly that word rolls off your tongue. I'm giving you fair warning—don't let the word *select* deceive you!

When you know the look, the feel, and the price per pound, the next decision is how much to buy. A strong trend in the markets today is for smaller portions in both the restaurants and the home. I believe this trend is here to stay, and that's okay. My point is to keep that smaller portion delicious. Go ahead and order that steak but eliminate those globs of butter and sour cream from your baked potato, order your salad dressing light, and you'll end up eating less fat in the trade-off. With that in mind, here are some guidelines for you to follow when purchasing meat.

1. 1/4 to 1/3 pound of boneless beef per person (one pound would serve three to four people).

2. 1/3 to 1/2 pound per person for steak or roast with minimum bone (one pound would serve two to three people).

3. 1/2 to 3/4 pound for a bone-in, standing rib roast or short ribs (figure one or two ribs per person, depending on size of rib and appetites).

4. 1/4 pound per person for ground beef (four 4-ounce patties per pound, uncooked; closer to 3-ounce cooked).

The health magazines and some cookbooks say to think of the size of a deck of cards for a cooked meat serving (after shrinkage, with no waste such as bone or fat). This is roughly three ounces. We all vary greatly in size, and it irks me when the fat fanatics tell

— BEEF
Where They

RIB
Rib Roast, Large End
Rib Roast, Small End
Rib Steak, Small End
Rib Eye Steak
Rib Eye Roast
Back Ribs

CHUCK
Chuck Eye Roast, Boneless
Top Blade Steak, Boneless
Arm Pot Roast
Shoulder Pot Roast, Boneless
Mock Tender Roast
Blade Roast
Under Blade Pot Roast
7-Bone Pot Roast
Short Ribs
Flanken-Style Ribs
Cross Rib Pot Roast

RIB

CHUCK

BRISKET

PLATE

SHANK

BRISKET
Whole Brisket
Brisket, Point Half, Corned
Brisket, Flat Half

PLATE
Skirt Steak

SHANK
Shank Cross Cut

*Beef primals that feature cuts lowest in fat.

CUTS —
Come From

SHORT LOIN*
Top Loin Steak, Boneless
T-Bone Steak
Porterhouse Steak
Tenderloin Roast/Steak

SIRLOIN*
Top Sirloin Steak
Sirloin Steak
Tenderloin Roast/Steak
Beef Tri-Tip
The tri-tip roast is a boneless cut from the bottom sirloin. It is also called a "triangle" roast because of its shape.

ROUND*
Round Steak
Top Round Roast
Top Round Steak
Bottom Round Roast
Tip Roast Cap Off
Eye Round Roast
Tip Steak
Boneless Rump Roast

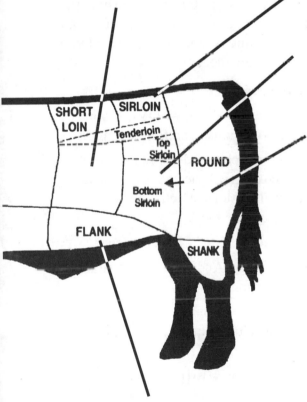

FLANK *
Flank Steak
Flank Steak Rolls

Courtesy of the Beef Industry Council—A division of the National Live Stock and Meat Board

us we can only eat three ounces. Does this mean a well-muscled, 220-pound man eats the same as a 110-pound woman?

If you're cooking for two, try selecting a strip, T-bone, or filet steak. For four you might elect to choose a thick porterhouse, and for six or more, try a big roast or a marinated flank steak. (See the recipe section.) You should also consider what you're serving with the meat. If you have a salad, potatoes or other starchy food, a cooked vegetable, bread, and dessert, you're going to need less meat per serving than if you just serve it with salad and bread.

Here's another option: buying beef by the side (half the animal) or by the quarter (front or rear with the better cuts, but you'll pay more). It will come cut and wrapped in the sizes you specify. Before you do this, consider these:

1. Do you have adequate freezer space?

2. Is your family large enough and do they LOVE ground beef and beef stew prepared a thousand different ways?

3. Buy an alarm for the freezer which sounds when the power goes off. More sophisticated ones will electronically call an alarm company. Check your insurance policy to see if a freezer full of thawed food is covered.

4. Be sure to buy the right grade of beef—high choice.

5. Take the whole family to Stuart Anderson's Restaurant for dinner with some of the money you'll save.

6. Buying meat that's on sale can actually save you more money than buying it by the side or quarter, and you get the cuts you want.

7. And lastly, this thought—eternity is two people and a side of beef!

Our beef industry has reacted to consumers' desires to lower fat intake by raising leaner beef. This makes sense; however, there are too many cattle going to market *too* lean, and they're ending up in the supermarket. This move to leaner cattle is progressive, but it's made it more difficult for the grocery shopper to buy a delicious piece of finely marbled meat with the great taste we all want. Sometimes I believe supermarkets are promoting leaner cuts of beef since it's about all they can get in today's market.

Brand names are on most dry goods and processed meats in the supermarket. Produce, pork, and most poultry are frequently being sold under brand names but are not graded. The grading system for beef is meant to assist the consumer in determining quality, but what's available at the meat counter may be the low end of *choice*. As a one-time cattle feeder, I found it made good economic sense to feed market animals just enough to grade *choice* and no more. This certainly doesn't help the consumer who's trying to buy quality beef. I feel this seventy-year old grading system has seen its day and privatization of quality beef will soon replace it. This practice will not only reward the cow/calf operators and feeders with higher prices for better beef, but it will also benefit the consumer because the quality will be guaranteed. The beef industry is just starting to sell some products by brand name, such as *Certified Angus Beef,* but in the meantime, I want you to be able to make intelligent selections without relying on confusing names, shapes, marketing ploys, and so forth.

Support the supermarket you're comfortable with. The market realizes that if they get your meat business, they're more than likely to get all your grocery money. They know the trend is away from fatty meat, so the good marketers are caught between a rock and a hard *beef*. They want to satisfy the customer's search for less fat, but after taking it home for dinner and trying to chew it, they also know he or she might not be back again—and, in my case, they're right. Let's not let the fat patrol force us into a life of suffering from being deprived of the greatest of all foods. A little much? Well, it's true!

Now, using the tips from this chapter, don't pick up the beef with the negatives I mentioned above. Use the positives and reduce the fat by serving well-trimmed, slightly smaller portions. You'll have taste and tenderness—the best of both worlds.

Would I rather give up my beef or my liberty? Let's see . . . the cogs are turning. Beef or liberty? Personally, I need my beef fix at least four or five times a week. Beef is a highly dense, nutritious entree, and, unlike carbohydrates, it satisfies for hours after you've eaten and keeps the hunger pains away. Most Americans love their beef with a passion. It's the most complete source of protein that exists, and it includes iron, minerals, and vitamins. To get the full benefit, you need to buy it fresh, prepare it properly, and savor it while eating it slowly. It will become the foundation of your weight-control program and long life. Many more older meat-eaters exist in this nation than old vegetarians! This statement is true but mis-leading, and I'm guilty of fooling with your head. Obviously, people eating meat outnumber vegetarians by a great deal. So there you have it.

Remember, you can't draw sweet water from a foul well and you can't cook a great steak out of bad stock. Take care. Go for the inevitable submission to the pure joy of a steak with the taste you deserve.

ALL LABELS, WISE AND WONDERFUL

You see new labels on most items now. They help us make decisions for balancing and planning our diet to satisfy our nutritional needs. This is the kind of action the government should get involved in. They're not telling us what we should and shouldn't eat—just what's in it! They're letting us make our own decisions. The information on packages is taking the guess work out of good nutrition.

The labels appearing on most food packages list what are known as daily values (DVs). The DVs for a 2000-calorie allowance are printed on each label and list the percentage of your daily allowances contained in that particular product. Of course, not everyone requires that exact amount. I use a 2200-calorie diet, so I just adjust the daily values up by ten percent and it works.

The new labels, as of 1994, tell consumers a great deal about some thirty thousand items in the supermarkets. Certain types of food are exempt: those without nutrients such as coffee, tea, most spices, and so forth; items served directly to you from a deli or bakery; and some other minor commodities. Fresh fruits and vegetables obviously cannot be individually labeled, but the information should be posted above the produce at the supermarket.

Other food items not requiring nutritional labels come in packages with less than twelve square inches of available space. There's no room for the new label; however, these products must have a phone number and/or address where you can get that information, if you so desire.

Study the percentage of the vitamins A and C halfway down the labels as they tend to be low in the average American diet. Also be aware of the serving size at the top of the label. New labeling methods have become more realistic, but the Food and Drug Administration (FDA) sets these sizes, and they're not necessarily what you and I eat at one sitting. Don't kid yourself when counting calories or fat grams—you could be getting more than you think if you're not taking that serving size into consideration.

These federal regulations have given new meaning to such abused marketing claims as "fat free" and "low calorie." "Free," "No," or "Zero" indicate that the product has nothing which could significantly affect your diet. Following are some definitions you might find of interest:

Cholesterol per serving:

"*Cholesterol Free*" means the product has two milligrams or less.

"*Low Cholesterol*" must have twenty milligrams or less.

Fat per serving:

"*Fat Free*" must have less than one-half (0.5) a gram.

"*Low Fat*" must have three grams or less.

"*Low Saturated Fat*" must have one gram or less.

Sodium per serving:

"Sodium Free" must have less than five milligrams.

"Low Sodium" must have one hundred and forty milligrams or less.

"Very Low Sodium" must have thirty-five milligrams or less.

Calories per serving:

"Low Calorie" must have forty calories or less.

"Reduced," *"less,"* and *"fewer"* mean the product has been nutritionally changed and now contains twenty-five percent less of a given nutrient or twenty-five percent fewer calories than the regular product.

"Light" means the product contains thirty-three percent fewer calories or fifty percent less fat than the regular product, or it can mean the salt (sodium) content is reduced by fifty percent. ("Light" is sometimes on a package to describe a light color of the product—this is permissible.)

A beef label should state where on the animal the cut comes from and the retail name.

"Well, what about beef and all other meat and seafood?" you're probably asking. Stay with me on this.

The USDA regulates meat—not the FDA. The USDA will be employing the same style of labels as the FDA, but considering the problem with sizing, it's now done by posting the information close to the market's meat counters. It will be similar to the one following. If you don't see the charts or brochures, ask for them.

"Lean" and "Extra-lean" describe the fat content of all meat, poultry, and seafood. "Lean" means less than ten grams of fat, four grams of saturated fat, and ninety-five milligrams of cholesterol per serving. "Extra-lean" means less than five grams of fat, two grams

BEEF
NUTRI-FACTS
UPDATE

BEEF NUTRITION FACTS

1/8" fat trim / trimmed of visible fat — BEEF, 3 oz cooked serving	Calories	Calories From Fat	Total Fat (g)	Saturated Fat (g)	Cholesterol (mg)	Sodium (mg)	Protein (g)	Iron (%DV)
Ground Beef, broiled, well done (10% fat*)	210	100	11	4	85	70	27	15
Ground Beef, broiled, well done (17% fat*)	230	120	13	5	85	70	24	15
Ground Beef, broiled, well done (27% fat*)	250	150	17	6	85	80	23	15
Brisket, Whole, braised	290 / 210	190 / 100	21 / 11	8 / 4	80 / 80	55 / 60	22 / 25	10 / 15
Chuck, Arm Pot Roast, braised	260 / 180	160 / 60	18 / 7	7 / 3	85 / 85	50 / 55	24 / 28	15 / 20
Chuck, Blade Roast, braised	290 / 210	190 / 100	21 / 11	9 / 4	90 / 90	55 / 60	23 / 26	15 / 15
Rib Roast, Large End, roasted	300 / 200	220 / 100	24 / 11	10 / 4	70 / 70	55 / 60	20 / 23	10 / 15
Rib Steak, Small End, broiled	280 / 190	190 / 90	21 / 10	9 / 4	70 / 70	55 / 60	20 / 24	10 / 10
Top Loin, Steak, broiled	230 / 180	130 / 70	15 / 8	6 / 3	65 / 65	55 / 60	22 / 24	10 / 10
Loin, Tenderloin Steak, broiled	240 / 180	150 / 80	16 / 9	6 / 3	75 / 70	50 / 55	22 / 24	15 / 15
Loin, Sirloin Steak, broiled	210 / 170	110 / 60	12 / 6	5 / 2	75 / 75	55 / 55	24 / 26	15 / 15
Eye Round, Roast, roasted	170 / 140	60 / 40	7 / 4	3 / 2	60 / 60	50 / 55	24 / 25	10 / 10
Bottom Round, Steak, braised	220 / 180	110 / 60	12 / 7	5 / 2	80 / 80	40 / 45	25 / 27	15 / 15
Round, Tip Roast, roasted	190 / 160	90 / 50	10 / 6	4 / 2	70 / 70	55 / 55	23 / 24	15 / 15
Top Round, Steak, broiled	180 / 150	70 / 40	7 / 4	3 / 1	70 / 70	50 / 50	26 / 27	15 / 15

Not a significant source of total carbohydrate, dietary fiber, sugars, vitamin A, vitamin C, and calcium.

Serving Size: 3 oz. cooked portion, without added fat, salt or sauces.

Developed By: Food Marketing Institute, American Dietetic Association, American Meat Institute, National-American Wholesale Grocers' Association, National Broiler Council, National Fisheries Institute, National Grocers Association, National Live Stock and Meat Board, National Turkey Federation, United Fresh Fruit and Vegetable Association.

Reviewed By: United States Department of Agriculture

Data Source: USDA Handbook 8-13, revised 1990 and Bulletin Board, 1994 (beef) and USDA Handbook 8-17, 1989 (veal)

3/95

of saturated fat, and ninety-five milligrams of cholesterol. (By the way, there are a thousand milligrams in a gram.)

Just one more point on the wise and wonderful labels. Hang in!

Most supermarkets are using a decimal system instead of pounds and ounces on meat labels to further confuse us. The decimal system states weight by indicating it on a scale of one to one hundred; for example, 1.0 would be one pound, 0.25 would be a quarter pound, 0.70 would be seven-tenths of a pound, and so forth.

Use all these labels and weights to calculate your daily allowance of calories, carbohydrates, and fat grams. Personalize your diet so you'll get good nutrition, but don't sacrifice taste. Follow that formula and the flavor of that steak will let your taste buds sing.

CHAPTER 14

THAT'S NOT GOOD FOR YOU, YOU KNOW

I'll tell you something that's not good. We, the American people, are the fattest people in the world and getting fatter. A Harris Poll found fifty-eight percent of Americans were overweight in 1983, sixty-four percent in 1990, and sixty-nine percent in 1994. From the Harvard School of Medicine: "Obesity is an alarming epidemic." Obesity is defined as twenty percent over your ideal weight. Twenty years ago, one out of every four of us was considered obese; now, one out of every three of us is. During that period, on average, each individual's weight increased eight pounds.

Again, during that same stretch of years, **our consumption of beef went from ninety pounds per person *DOWN* to seventy pounds**. The number of cows on the land went from a hundred and thirty-five million in 1975 to a hundred and three million in 1995 (figures from the *1996 Information Please Almanac*). The nation's consumption of vegetable fats has tripled. I'm not drawing any conclusions—that's not my job—BUT the above facts will give you something to think about. Are the food police pointing us in the wrong direction?

How about this: When we were becoming fatter and fatter, the diet centers, such as Weight Watchers™, Jenny Craig™, and so forth, were all building into big businesses—thirty-two **billion** dollars a year and growing. Have you gone to a bookstore lately and checked out the cookbook and health sections? It's diet-this and diet-that. Exercise centers have more than doubled and we have become extremely conscious of that nasty, three-letter word—FAT. Go down the aisle in the supermarket and all you see is "Low Fat," "No Fat," and "Less Fat." You never see "Lots of fat for the buck!" I try to find an upside to everything, but all I could come up with here was: "You'll see a lot of fat men leading a parade, but you'll never see a fat man leading a riot."

Our life expectancy took a downturn for the first time in a long time in 1993 (latest available figures). According to Metropolitan Life Insurance Company, the average life expectancy for Americans went to 75.4, down from 75.7 in 1992. This decline was the largest in decades. Despite constantly improving medical care, this dip has gone unexplained.

I wish I had a dollar for every time I've read or heard some so-called expert on "healthy" eating say, "Avoid red meat and eat skinless chicken or fish instead." Nutritionally, skinless chicken and lean beef are very similar—the skinless dark meat of chicken actually has more calories and fat than beef. When defending beef, the next thing you usually hear is, "Maybe so, but there's a lot more saturated fat in beef." The saturated fat in cooked lean beef is about thirty-nine percent and in skinless roasted chicken it's twenty-eight percent (turkey is thirty-three percent). Chicken is slightly *higher* than beef in cholesterol. Chicken has only ten to twelve percent of the vitamin B12 found in red meat and has smaller amounts of other minerals also, such as zinc. There's really no comparison with chicken the way it's usually eaten, fried with the skin on. Chicken wings this way have 328 calories in four ounces, which is more than a four-ounce choice tenderloin, and has twenty-two grams of total fat compared to the tenderloin's sixteen. You should also watch the seafood you eat. Shrimp has more than twice the cholesterol of an equal-weight serving of beef. Salmon has 9.3 grams of fat versus lean beef's 8.4, and it's almost identical in cholesterol content. This is what I'm talking about when I say, "Beef is getting a bum steer!"

If you're in the food business, and basically we all are because we eat to survive, you should follow studies and research on diet, which are enough to drive you nuts. (My wife says that's a short trip for me.) We all look to these studies to assist us in our desire for a long, healthy life. The government's responsibility is to protect us from false claims and tainted food—not telling us what to eat. The "experts" keep changing their damned minds, and anyway, they always conclude their latest report with that overused phrase— "More research is needed." To perpetuate their paycheck is why more research is needed. Why don't they do the "more" and then tell us the results?

Remember the raves about oats and oat bran and how they would increase your sex drive? I was about ready to seed half the ranch to oats (not just for me, you understand), then further research made a mockery of the first study. I'm sure glad I didn't get around to planting those dumb oats. I think we all remember the butter research. A good portion of us switched to margarine, and the restaurants went to a combination of spreads. Margarine, you see, has no cholesterol. Then it was discovered (next study) that margarine has trans-fatty acids (TFAs). TFAs can raise blood levels of *bad* cholesterol and lower the *good* cholesterol. In further studies by Drs. Walter Willett and Alberto Ascherio, they concluded that, gram for gram, TFAs contribute even more to the risk of heart disease than the saturated fats in meat and dairy products. So, back to butter— thank God! I personally couldn't stand the odor or texture of most brands of margarine.

There was a debate about shark steak and cranberries being dangerous, then they tried to convince us we'd die of Alar poisoning if we ate apples (a real bum rap for the apple industry), then the caffeine in coffee, followed by the chemicals in decaf. A big warning came out in 1996 about California strawberries causing cyclospora, then we saw a follow-up in *Newsweek* that flippantly stated, "Sorry, wrong berry. . . ." It was raspberries from Guatemala. In the meantime, what happened to the poor California strawberry farmers during their peak season? Pick yourself up, dust yourself off, and start all over again. Too much! The press should take the time to double-check stories for accuracy. Read the article on the right from a California newspaper.

I never raised hogs or pigs in my life, and I doubt the Duke did either. Nothing wrong with it, and thanks to those hog farmers, I can enjoy a good pork roast or chop. But the article has its facts all screwed up. The media's search for truth is complicated by:

- Authors of medical journals seeking prestige
- Scientists trying to obtain fame and grants
- The reading public's overwhelming desire for good health
- Newspapers turning inconclusive research into attention-getting stories
- Environmentalists seeking profit or support for their cause

Whatever the latest media hype is, we react, and I'm not sure this craving for knowledge on our part is always in our own best interest. Back and forth we go; does chlorine cause breast cancer, is there an association between hot dogs and childhood leukemia, what does beta carotene do to the lungs? The list goes on. Nothing seems to be proven with further research. Most of these studies are done for our protection, but they should be sure of the results and not reported prematurely without a strong backup of facts! I might add that the majority of these studies are done at your expense.

Previous studies have claimed that fish is good for the heart. Now a new (1995) study at Harvard shows that "It doesn't hurt, but it doesn't help the heart . . . further study is needed." How did they arrive at this theory in the first place? The Japanese have a longer life span than Americans and less heart trouble; they eat a lot of fish, but not a lot of beef, so they just assumed that was the answer. Some study! Somalians have an extremely short life span of fifty-six years and they have little or zero beef in their diet. In India it's fifty-nine years, and because they consider beef animals sacred, they cannot be eaten. What's this mean? Not a damn thing! But it is the kind of statistic some people use to prove their point. Their life span is less, but many conditions enter into that fact.

▶ A 6,000-acre bed-and-breakfast ranch gives city slickers a chance to ride into the past without leaving too many creature comforts behind.

By Gordon Johnson
The Press-Enterprise

SAGE

The trail snaked around clumps of white sage, thorny cactus and yucca stalks crowned with yellow blooms, squeezing the motley band of riders into single file.

Just ahead, a woman in crisp Wranglers moved nicely with the paddle-footed, parade gait of her Peruvian Paso horse.

Then, without warning, she grabbed her hat by its brim, leaned sharply to the left and waved it at a small lizard on the trail, trying to shoo it from advancing horse hooves.

"You better get moving, little fellow," she said in a voice sweet enough to calm a child after a nightmare.

Surely, this was a first. A cowhand worried about a lizard on the trail?

But then, city slickers are like that.

They had come — a half dozen of them — from the wilds of Simi Valley and Mission Viejo and San Pedro to work cattle on Rancho Pavoreal, a 6,000-acre bed-and-breakfast ranch east of Temecula and south of Hemet, where dudes eat dust by day and filet mignon by night.

They had come to get a taste of the Old West, but a comfortable taste. They had come to the right place.

The ranch's main house is long and low with a front porch that runs the length of it. Big picture windows overlook the brushy valley where cattle and coyotes roam. In the distance, Mt. Palomar rises to meet the clouds, with its white-domed observatory sticking out like a fly on a birthday cake.

Pavoreal means peacock in Spanish, but there isn't a peacock in sight. Instead, white geese waddle the grounds, greeting visitors with indignant honks. When not guarding the place, they feed in the large pond below the house along with ducks, bullfrogs and mosquito fish.

Next to the house is the huge pool that John Wayne built. "The Duke" owned the ranch from about 1938 to 1949. He and his partner, Stuart Anderson of steak house fame, raised hogs at Rancho Pavoreal, and cattle at their Red River Ranch in Arizona.

But more than a livestock ranch,

it was a getaway lodge where Wayne's buddies like Andy Devine, Gabby Hayes and Gene Autry would fly in for a few days of pleasure riding and lounging around the pool.

Allen and Joanne Senall took over the ranch in 1989 after it had been abandoned for more than 20 years. Hippies and other transients had wrecked the house, but a year and a half of hard work restored it to its former glory.

Now Allen runs the ranch and Joanne takes care of the bed-and-breakfast end of the operation.

Please see RANCH, C-4

One example of a great reversal I was tickled to read about was in Dietary Guidelines released recently by the government which stated that "moderate alcohol consumption offers certain health benefits." "No further research is needed."—*S. Anderson* Five years earlier, the official government Dietary Guidelines said: "Drinking alcohol has no net health benefits and is not recommended." I much prefer the official stand of 1995, but do they really know what it's all about? At a recent news conference, Dr. Lee, U.S. Assistant Secretary of Health, explained, "To move from anti-alcohol to health benefits is a big change." I should think so! Now they cite numerous studies reporting the cardiovascular benefits linked with moderate consumption of alcohol. Is it scientific, or at some point does science give way and mystery take over? Oh, happy day. But I must remind myself of that undefined term— MODERATION. I can't adopt that "one-size-fits-all" attitude. No single rule works for every free-living human being. Enjoy your drink, and here's a toast to your good health.

We Americans are changing our diets constantly to conform. Since the mid-seventies, we've built up to a carbo craze. It's interesting to note that the giant food companies are among the chief funders of nutritional research and these food companies are into selling junk and "healthy" carbos because it's big business. According to the food Nazis, we are suppose to eat unlimited carbos, cut the meat protein, and get what we need from tofu, soybeans, or peanut butter. Are they kidding? Soy beans? "Healthy food is like the food they serve in hell," says Henry Beard, a well-known chef. Could this be "hell-thy food?" I'll go along with him. This craze isn't working.

If you're on the carbohydrate bandwagon, ask yourself these questions: Don't you find you're hungry before it's time for the next meal? Do you catch yourself cheating and lacking your normal energy? Somebody said, "All that vegetarians eat are side dishes." Or how about this one: "I find meat-eaters are much less violent than vegetarians." I didn't say that, Ghandi did. I don't mean to pick on vegans, I respect their right to eliminate animal products from their diet. I just wish they, in turn, respected my right to eat meat. No less an authority than the American Heart Association has stated: "If you thought a cholesterol-lowering diet meant giving up red meat, you'll be pleased to know it's an unnecessary sacrifice."

> *The man who does not eat everything*
> *must not condemn the man*
> *who does, for God has accepted him. . . .*
>
> *Romans 14:3*

Food plays a major role in our existence—three meals a day, every day of our lives—and it should be looked forward to. For the majority of us this includes red meat and to say meat's not good for us or meant to be eaten is nonsense. We are carnivores. The design of our teeth is proof of that. The big fish eat the little fish in the ocean. The ecological balance of nature depends on animals eating other animals. Our earliest relatives from eons ago survived on meat and maybe a few roots and berries. Now we are they. There were no crops in those early days, but they survived. Thank God for that or none of us would be here.

THE SUMMER OF OUR DISCONTENT

In the summer of 1993, hundreds got sick from a strain of E-coli and three people died in the Seattle area. The three deaths can't compare to the thousands we lose to accidents and violence each year, but it's three too many, and we need to act now! Americans have the safest food supply in the world, and we just don't think of people dying from what they've eaten. It shouldn't happen, but it did, and we can make it safer.

In the summer of 1996, E-coli hit thousands in Japan with seven deaths. The source of this epidemic at this date has been determined to be radish sprouts. I've never heard of this dish and it wouldn't be very high on my list of wants. But this sad occurrence does bring to light the fact E-coli can happen anywhere, at any time, and from unexpected sources. E-coli is particularly dangerous to children and older people and can be found in uncooked hamburger and many other foods. It has been discovered in shellfish and even seaweed. Earlier suspects in Japan were sea eel sushi, tuna paste, and tea. Vegetables are not immune either.

We as individual operators, as well as all the meat associations, are constantly working in cooperation with the government toward one hundred percent purity, one hundred percent of the time. You should know that the beef producers have spent more than five million dollars just since 1992 to support and fund new research that will safeguard against E-coli and other harmful bacteria and improve food safety processes and procedures. As business people, it's the smart thing to do. They have instigated studies with experts and have invited health officials to work with them.

In July 1996 President Clinton signed a bill that approved widespread changes in the meat and poultry inspection system. Under the new edict, processing plants will be required to implement a scientific-based procedure to prevent contamination. No more "just sniff and poke." These improvements will be coming about in stages over the next three years. The USDA has approved the use of a steam pasteurization process for fresh beef that meets the "zero tolerance" requirement in eliminating pathogenic bacteria, including E-coli (developed by private agri-businesses and funded by the beef associations). This valuable new technology, called high-temperature vacuuming, works by passing the carcass through a steam or hot water chamber and then vacuuming the moisture from the surface of the carcass. By the end of April, 1996, the plants that process eighty-five percent of all U.S. fed cattle were voluntarily using the system. It would have been one hundred percent, but the manufacturers couldn't make them fast enough. Everyone involved in this industry, including the government, has a clear-cut obligation to ensure that tainted chicken and other meats (or food of any type) don't reach the consumer.

Our in-house health department's biggest no-no is to leave any meat product out on the counter. Either the handler must be in the process of cutting and trimming the meat or cooking it. It must be kept cold (40 degrees or less) or hot and held over or under 140-degree heat, with no exceptions. Food-borne illness is easily prevented by properly handling, cooking, and storing food.

From the farm to the kitchen the possibility exists for contamination of meat, but once it gets to your kitchen, there's no excuse for food-caused illnesses. Here are some proper meat-handling rules:

- Keep meat cold or hot—less than 40 or higher than 140 degrees.
- Heat to the proper internal temperature—hamburgers should be 160 degrees or have all pink color gone. See the charts in Chapter 17 for steaks and roasts.
- Refrigerate leftovers within two hours after cooking.
- Take an ice chest with you in hot weather for food that can spoil rapidly if you know you're not going straight home after shopping.
- Never thaw frozen perishable foods at room temperature.
- Don't put hot foods in very large containers in the refrigerator or freezer as they can heat the interior of your appliance to dangerous levels. Let food adequately cool and put in smaller-sized containe ` so it can cool faster.
- Scour cutting boards thoroughly before and after using with meat, fish or eggs.
- Use germ-resistant sponges or paper towels for cleanup.
- Don't reuse utensils or dishes that have been used with raw meat.
- After handling raw meat, wash your hands with an antibacterial soap.

A professor of microbiology, Dr. Gerba, has shown that, after handling raw meat, washing your hands and cleaning up the work area with antibacterial soap and using paper towels that are thrown away could prevent ninety percent (that's a lot) of all food-borne illness. Dishcloths and most sponges (you can buy germ-*resistant* sponges) are often infected with salmonella, staphylococcus, and other disease-causing germs.

The reason hamburger or other ground meats can become contaminated is because they are ground up. This can spread bacteria inside the meat where the heat doesn't reach them if left rare. This is not true of roasts and steaks. As long as the surface temperatures are adequate to eliminate the bacteria, you do not need to ruin them by overcooking.

The latest findings show that an old-fashioned butcher-block cutting board is more sanitary than the newer plastic boards. That was our thinking all along. Place your *wood* board in the microwave on high for five minutes to sterilize it (be sure there's no metal on it and check it periodically because it will start to burn after three minutes if there's no moisture in the wood). Rub baking soda on the wood surface to help cleanse it. Rubbing it with onion also kills germs. After cutting something with a strong odor such as garlic or onion, rub it with a freshly cut lemon. Put your *plastic* board in the dishwasher to sterilize those deep scratches (microwaving doesn't work here because there's no moisture).

About the worst thing that can happen to a restaurant, and sometimes it's the death knell, is a published closure for lack of sanitation. We all lived in constant dread that one of our twelve stores would have just one crew member fail in his sanitation duties and get some unwanted space in the paper. Deep caca! Real deeeep caca!

In discussing this potential with Bruce Attebery, I said, "Why don't we start our own department of health?" He was all for it, and, shortly after, interviewed a gal for an office position in our growing chain. He felt she might be a prospect to head our new environmental department. Beverly McMillan exuded efficiency.

She was young, well dressed, and confident. Her lack of shyness was an asset, and I felt she had the strength to handle this new job. Definitely not the type who would blend into an empty room.

Before hiring her, I again talked with Bruce. I suggested we ask her to take us to her home right then so we could see how really neat and clean she was. He said, "Now, isn't that an invasion of privacy?" I thought for a second and decided he was right—that's something David Letterman would do. I've often wondered what her abode was like that day, but I bet it would've passed inspection.

Beverly became known as "Susie Spotless" and our new department went into action. We asked the health department if Bev could accompany the local inspectors on their rounds. They were more than glad to do it and she got some excellent schooling.

The managers grew to fear a visit from Susie (also referred to as Gloria Glitter) more than they ever did from the local inspectors. The reports that Bev returned had an effect on the evaluations for their bonuses. To this day the kitchens reflect her efforts, even though she has long since moved on.

Let me leave this chapter on what's not good for you with something that is—chocolate with red wine. That's right! Both treats contain phenols which are chemicals believed to help stop arteries from clogging up. Andrew Waterhouse and colleagues at the University of California at Davis sent these results to the *Lancet Medical Journal* in the summer of 1996. Now, doesn't that make us all feel better!

FLASH: We have another serious outbreak of E-coli on the West coast as we go to press and it's caused by **Odwalla apple juice**. Odwalla is a good company and very upset over this incident, cooperating totally, and stating they only used picked apples which they scrubbed thoroughly before processing. (This means no apples were taken off the ground which eliminates animal contamination–how many orchards do you see with fences around them for livestock?) Like the beef industry, here's another business that takes every precaution possible and pride in its product, yet something like this happens. This is a rude awakening to the vegetarians who thought they were immune to such problems. The experts now tell us that we should be very careful with rice, tofu, melons, seafood, any product not pasteurized, and unwashed vegetables or fruits. Again I say, **practice sanitation**–it's all in the handling of the product! Wash anything you eat in its raw form thoroughly and wash your hands and utensils in between working with different foods. I know I'm repetitious, but contamination can be stopped by cleanliness and good sanitation. And remember, the concern about E-coli from unpasteurized apple juice does not translate into a concern for fresh apples picked from the tree. The apple growers have had enough unfair and negative press already.

CHAPTER 15

SO YOU'RE INTO COUNTING FAT GRAMS?

If you think meat is your largest source of fat, think again. The main villains are oils, butter, margarine, salad dressing, whole milk, and creams. If your spouse wants a Big Mac at McDonald's, but all you're going to have is a salad with a packet of bleu cheese, you are consuming more fat than your spouse. That's right. Fast-food places are not necessarily the fat dives that the food police want you to think they are. Junk food? Meat, milk, and potatoes? No. I'll tell you what's junk. It's drugs, cigarettes, and turnips.

You can't eliminate all fat from your diet and survive. **The body can't make fatty acids—it must get it from food.** You need it to live and be healthy. It would be very difficult and undesirable to try to avoid all fat. Fat supplies the essential fatty acids which are crucial for growth and development and protects us against starvation and extreme weather conditions. Fat components are used to maintain cell membranes, regulate cholesterol, and produce vital hormones. When eaten, fat makes you feel full so your body signals you to *stop*. (This is a big deal for me!) It stays with you longer because of the digestion time, so you're not looking for snacks shortly after your meal. (This is another big help for me, and I need all the help I can get.) Fat also helps transport vitamins A, D, E, and K throughout your body. Eating less than fifteen percent fat of your total allowable calories can result in vitamin and mineral deficiencies. One more point the ladies especially like: Fat helps maintain beautiful and healthy skin and hair.

If you're into counting fat grams, I can work with that. Even the proponents of high-protein/low-carbohydrate diets would agree that the current consumption of thirty-seven-percent fat is high, and this should be cut to thirty percent. So I have no quarrel with diet gurus who recommend lowering our intake. I just don't think we should have to give up our favorite foods to do it. In *The Zone,* which at this writing has been on the *New York Times' Bestseller List* the entire summer of 1996, author Dr. Barry Sears recommends thirty percent fats, thirty percent protein, and forty percent carbohydrates and makes a convincing argument against the so-called "healthy diet" recommendation of 15/15/70. In case you haven't figured it out, there's a diet war going on out there, and these books are bringing the battle into the open.

There are several recent books (1995-1996) by doctors who agree with this balanced-diet theory in which less carbohydrates are eaten, and I refer you to these experts in this complex business. I don't have enough initials behind my name and can only report studies and statistics. They all agree you should be able to eat some of the fatty food you love—just limit the portions and eat foods in the proper balance. I've included quotes from the book covers on the following list:

The Zone by Barry Sears, Ph.D. (Regan Books): "The new dietary recommendations of the U.S. government, nutrition experts, and medical experts are dead wrong."

Protein Power by Drs. Michael and Mary Dan Eades (Bantam Books): "If you eat too little protein, as you do on most low-fat diets, your body begins to cannibalize its muscles—including the heart."

Dr. Atkins' New Health Revolution by Robert Atkins, M.D., sold over five million copies (Bantam Books): "Offers readers a powerful new program based on a low-carbohydrate/low-sugar diet."

Healthy For Life, a bestseller by Drs. Richard and Rachael Heller (A Plume Book): ". . . you may be carbohydrate sensitive and snacking on 'healthy' low-fat foods such as breads, pasta, fruits, and even carrots, cottage cheese, and yogurt may actually increase your chances for weight gain, serious illness, and early death."

These diets are really the result of the work that's been done with eicosanoids (pronounced eye-KAH-sah-noids). Early discoveries in this research won the 1982 Nobel Prize for Medicine. Very briefly, hormones such as insulin and glucagon control blood sugar and eicosanoids control the hormones. As Dr. Sears puts it: "They're the molecular glue that holds the human body together." Dietary fat is the only source of the essential fatty acids that are the chemical building blocks for all eicosanoids.

There is even a new study that cancer research has reported on a fatty acid that seems to inhibit breast cancer in rats. This acid (CLA) is found in animal foods such as red meat and dairy products. The report (*American Institute for Cancer Research Newsletter*, Summer, 1994, Issue 44) does conclude that further research is needed. Sophisticated research conducted throughout the country recently has led to new theories. It's been proven that, whether simple or complex, a carbohydrate is a carbohydrate, and they convert to sugar. A diet heavy on carbohydrates (more than forty percent) might be contributing to the obesity problems in this country.

I'm reminded of a cartoon in which a very obese man is saying: "I don't understand it, I keep gaining weight. The only snacks I've had today are a dozen nonfat cookies, a quart of nonfat ice cream, a package of nonfat pretzels, four bowls of nonfat cereal with nonfat milk and sugar." Of course, he's going to gain and gain because he's not counting calories! That's still necessary to control your weight.

Lower your fat intake in areas where taste is not that important to you. For instance, you can go to fat-free yogurt or try the new fat-free, butter-like spray. If butter is important to you, then stay with it and eliminate fat elsewhere, like fat-free or low-fat mayonnaise, or the new fat-free desserts or ice cream. Remember, you still consider calories.

I don't go back as far as the horse-drawn milk wagon, but I remember hearing the rattle of the bottles as they were left on our family porch. The cream separated to the top of the bottle, and if left out too long in freezing weather, the cream would push the lid up an inch or two and stand frozen in place. Sometimes my father would shake the bottle, mixing the cream with the milk. Usually my mother took the cream off to use in their coffee or put on our cereal. Now, that's fat! But they weren't overweight.

Over the years, to help control calories and fat intake, I first went to two percent milk, then one percent, and finally nonfat. Now, during those rare times when we can only get one or two percent milk, it tastes like that old bottle of cream. It's an adjustment that milk drinkers can make without the loss of the nutritional benefits that milk gives. The correct one is whatever works for you. Friends of ours bring their own milk when they stay with us—they can't handle our *blue* skim milk. Everyone need not practice the same methods of lowering fat intake—there are many avenues to explore.

"Hey, kids, you want fries with that?" Certainly they do—kids just love French fries, just one reason the school food directors are finding it difficult to meet the new government regulations for their lunch program. These guidelines call for less fat and more fruit and vegetables. These mandates state that no more than thirty percent of calories can be from fat, and of that, only ten percent can be saturated fat. Sound familiar? Young or old, big or small, playing football or reading a book—everyone's treated the same. We're as different as our fingerprints. Gimme a break!

Remember, these are kids. Some day they'll grow up and get even!

What could be more American than a burger and fries? Don't try to make them off limits. We can work at this combination and make them a little less greasy. You can lessen the fat on those fries by lightly brushing with oil or butter after slicing them into an oil-sprayed pan and baking them. Use lean ground beef, no butter, and *light* mayonnaise on that hamburger. School cafeteria nutritionists found they have to give the kids taste or they'll bring their jam sandwiches and Twinkies from home. The school districts are asking for extensions on these guidelines with the main problem being that the kids won't or don't go for it. Many students are throwing their vegetables away or just not buying their lunches. There has been some success with disguising the broccoli with cheese, but that's self-defeating. Using extra-extra-lean ground beef can be like eating sawdust, and nonfat cheese like rubber. We have to be kid-friendly. Fat can be cut, but if you go too far, you cut taste and that's a mistake. We should take a lesson from McDonald's (where you'll probably find the kids buying a "real" lunch after they've run away from the cafeteria). They tried a McLean burger which should have been called the "McFlop;" after five years, the company gave up on it altogether because no one was buying it.

I remember a TV news program where a mother at a school-board meeting got all bent out of shape because her child was "exposed" to hamburger and fries at his school's cafeteria one day a week. We should monitor our children's nutrition but not overreact. We shouldn't lay unnecessary restrictions on our kids during those precious years we have them at home. Let's concern ourselves with the more critical problems at school: drugs, violence, auto accidents, and teen sex. Let's work on making the neighbor-hoods safe so they can walk to school and play without worry. Let's build bike paths, tennis courts, and more pools so they can play such strenuous sports as tennis and water polo and have places where more children can enjoy physical activities.

Where do we go from here? I recently read where the Center for Science in the Public's Interest has exposed the high fat content and calories in Chinese food, Mexican food, strict vegetarian fare, and deli sandwich shops. How many of you can go to a movie at a theater and not eat popcorn? They've tried to spoil that for us, too. Like we should be filled with guilt if we eat any of these things after seeing the numbers? To paraphrase a wise old saying, these should be taken with a gram of fat. They say a tuna salad sandwich has 833 calories and 58 grams of fat and an egg salad has 664 calories with 44 fat grams. Yet four ounces of water-packed tuna has two grams of fat and an egg has five and a half grams. Apparently these high fat counts are coming from the mayonnaise, butter, or other heavy add-ons. It makes good copy for the press not to consider the sandwich fillings made with very little, light mayo and water-packed tuna. They want to make us sit up and take notice or they don't consider it news.

Then we have our vegetarian sandwiches which can end up with as much fat, saturated and otherwise, as two quarter-pounders. The avocado, cheese, and mayo alone could add up to 753 calories and 40 fat grams. Linda McCartney's vegetarian burgers won't do you much good either—if you can find them. They were recalled after a TV program analyzed some of them and found a fat content of more than twenty percent—the package said 11.2 percent. How about a bowl of Quaker 100% Natural Cereal? One half cup contains almost four grams of saturated fat which is eighteen percent of your daily maximum, and that's just in half a cup. It's even more saturated fat than you'd get from a fast-food hamburger. This is taken from *Nutrition Action Healthletter*'s "10 Foods You Should Never Eat." Try the low-fat granola by Quaker or Kellogg's instead—or maybe that hamburger?

I'm not saying that counting your fat grams is a waste of time, but there are more important things in life. Eating is supposed to be a fun experience. Most of us do it at least three times each day of our lives and we don't want to evaluate every single thing we eat. Don't say good-bye to foods you love—just cut down on the amount. I would rather have a few bites of the real thing than triple the bites of foods from hell. How about just not cleaning everything off your plate? When it says "no fat" we pop it in and then we get heavier and wonder why. Calories in—calories out. *Out* means exercise.

I don't think anyone—authors, nutritionists, doctors, vegetarians, or meat lovers—would disagree on the following. It's the need for this tortured process we call exercise. It helps, and nobody doubts that, but should it be vigorous or moderate? Recently there's been some disagreement about this. The government's Center for Disease Control and Prevention has been suggesting walking as the key to long life. However, in a twenty-six-year study of Harvard alumni who graduated between 1924 and 1954, it was found moderate exercise didn't increase longevity. According to Dr. Lee, assistant professor of medicine at Harvard, only vigorous exercise is associated with lower mortality.

I raised more than cattle and horses on the ranch; I also had dogs, lots of dogs. The active ones all lived long lives. The last one was a cross between a collie and German shepherd named Shelly. She followed me whether I was on a bike, on horseback, or in a pickup—even when it was extremely hot. My point is that she enjoyed a long life for a large dog—almost eighteen years—because she exercised. She was so old she farted soot, but that great dog was in good condition. Maybe that's the answer to longevity. Here we go again with the big debates choose your weapons.

My brother jogs, so a few years back, I thought I should try it. It did it once and that was enough. Not for me! We came from the same pool of genes, so why the difference? Probably because we're all unique and as different from each other as our DNA. So, too, are our needs for diet and exercise. Erma Bombeck once said she would take up jogging again just to hear heavy breathing. I do exercise and enjoy most forms, and that's the key word—*enjoy*. Do what feels good to you.

I built a regulation squash court in the Black Angus headquarters' office building in the early seventies. I had it double-insulated so that if times got tough and we needed the space, it could easily be converted to a chill room for aging beef for the restaurants. For years, I got good exercise and enjoyment from that sport, as did lots of other staff members. It was vigorous but fun!

Doctors say exercise, not diet, is the key to fighting this growing obesity epidemic. It takes more calories to feed muscle than flab so we get to eat more. People expend less energy than their forefathers. We're probably eating about the same amount of food as our ancestors, but the big difference is they worked their butts off and we're basically sedentary. We don't climb stairs when we can take the escalator—we don't even roll up our windows in our cars anymore. We have TV remotes so we don't have to get off our asses. We'll go around the block three times to get a closer parking space to our destination. Wouldn't want to walk a couple of blocks—heaven forbid!

People associate eating out with pigging out, breaking your diet, or losing control of your fat-gram counting. It could happen but it doesn't have to. Any good cut of beef in a restaurant will probably be eight to ten ounces or more. Competitively, the operators have to satisfy the big appetite or jeopardize their customer base. Take a doggie bag home. All operators offer this service whether you have a dog or not. Don't forget and leave it in the car. It happens. You open your door a couple of days later and wonder, "What's that funny smell?" I remember my mother served leftovers for years and we teased her because we never did see the original.

Speaking for restaurateurs, I'll admit we're guilty to the degree of giving the customer too much food. Many customers expect the twelve- to sixteen-ounce prime rib, plus a big baked potato slathered with gobs of butter, sour cream, and bacon bits. How about adding a creamed soup and salad dressing to that, and to top everything off, a slice of mud pie with whipped cream? There are enough fat and calories there to last for days. If you're celebrating or this is a once-a-month treat, it won't kill you, so live it up!

Restaurants are willing to work with customers who are counting calories, so here's a summary of what you can do. First, use a doggie bag and take half your dinner home. You will now have more than enough for lunch tomorrow or another dinner. Another smart move is to order your salad dressing on the side and dip your fork in for each bite. You should save well over three-fourths of the normal serving size. Ask the server to hold the butter and cream and substitute a nonfat yogurt or similar dressing. Lots of operators will give you low-calorie offerings as replacements. It's a good idea to always ask how certain dishes are prepared. Steaks should be grilled, for example. Ask which roasts and steaks are leaner (again, beware of extra-lean). Give your server a break, however, and don't take too long agonizing over your choices. It's a waste of his or her time and time is the stuff life is made of.

The last tip I even hate to write, but if you don't want the calories that are in the mud pie—DON'T order it. I do, but then I'm a wild and crazy kinda guy.

Always check your ticket for mistakes even if it embarrasses your spouse or table mates—servers are human you know. And don't forget, the restaurant does the dishes. I'm not even involved anymore, but I can't stop putting plugs in.

The key is individualizing your diet to your body and situation: overall health, lifestyle, exercise habits, weight, bone structure, family history, blood pressure, cholesterol level, your likes and dislikes, and so forth. The foods you enjoy should be a part of your diet, even if they're in limited quantities.

If you're really anxious to look younger and slimmer, hang out with old, fat people!

SO YOU'RE INTO COUNTING
FAT GRAMS?

SECTION IV

COOKING BEEF

(IN THE KITCHEN)

CHAPTER 16

HEY, I'M
DOUBLE-PARKED HERE—
MOVE IT!

Hey, that's an outstanding selection of beef you just made! You don't have to double-park, but move it on home—don't go and do anything else. Don't blow it by not storing it right once you get it home. If you're going to use your purchase that day, leave it in the original package and immediately put it in the refrigerator. If it'll be a day or two, then rewrap it loosely in freezer paper (paper with a waxed side), place it on a plate or other container to catch any drippings, and set it in the coldest part of the refrigerator. Ground beef should be used within two days or else double-wrapped and frozen. If you're going to freeze meat, you should leave it in the original wrapper, but wrap it again with foil or plastic wrap—**be sure to label and date it**. It'll keep approximately four months this way. Incidentally, home vacuum-packaging systems are great and will keep your meat even longer. It's a good idea to buy a larger amount when you see those great sales and then repackage it into serving sizes to suit your family. Our vacuum-packer has more than paid for itself because it cuts down on spoilage in the freezer and pantry.

Freezing should take place as quickly as possible so packages should not be too large. When frozen too slowly, more juices will be lost during thawing, which is another reason for making smaller packages (two pounds or less). Thaw it in the refrigerator. Don't leave beef sitting out on the counter, and if you use the microwave for defrosting, use the *defrost* setting. Turn the meat over and keep it rotating so the microwave doesn't start cooking the meat in some areas. We bought a product sold via TV infomercials that defrosts meat faster. Just sit it on the tray, which you've preheated with hot water, and turn it after a few minutes (again heating the tray). A steak will defrost in less than half an hour this way. I'm not promoting the product, but it does seem to work.

In the restaurant business, the handling of meat must follow strict guidelines. Meat must always be refrigerated at forty degrees or less, or, if cooked, kept under the heat lamps or in a warming oven at one hundred and forty degrees or more. These rules must be followed by the kitchen crew. No exceptions! Suzy Spotless and the Health Department frown on any other practice.

Pay attention to the "use by" and "sell by" dates on the perishable products. The "use by" date applies to how long you can keep a product at home. It's important to remember that these dates refer to quality of food and are not guarantees that the food is not contaminated. "Use by" dates are suggestions. They don't necessarily mean you have to throw food out if expired. The date just gives fair warning.

If the "sell by" date has passed, don't buy it. If you've already bought it and the date has gone by, don't throw it away until you've checked it out. Use your new grading skills—smell, touch, and color. It might be good, but the same rules as above apply. You can also return it to the store with your dated sales slip so they'll know it was past its prime.

ADVERSITY IS OPPORTUNITY IN DISGUISE!

Did you hear about the cook who said he never made a mistake? He works for a restaurant that did!

How do we doctor the little (and sometimes big) mistakes we make? Let me count the ways. First, try to blame someone else! If that doesn't work, it could've been the equipment. If they don't believe this, then admit you didn't do it exactly right. You might even have to fess up to a total disaster—burn, baby, burn! I think anyone who's ever cooked can sing a few bars of that.

Here are some steps you can take when you scorch something. Speed is important in the following moves: Uncover and take the pan away from the source of heat. Quickly put some cold water in the sink and set the pan in it. (This is not normally recommended by the manufacturers as it could warp the pan, so you may want to evaluate how necessary the dish is to your overall meal or how close you are to the nearest restaurant. We've done this without harm to our pans.) Immediately separate the good part from the burned part and transfer it to another container. Taste it, and if it still gives off that burned odor, cover it with a damp cloth and let it sit awhile. Taste again and if the offending taste is still really strong, give up and chuck it. If it's borderline, the only possible solution is to make it into barbecued beef with a well-seasoned barbecue sauce. Do you suppose that's the source of some barbecued-beef lunch specials. Naw! There are times, through some tears, that you have to throw good food away.

After the burn, you're now faced with the cleanup and odor. Not to worry, just follow a few of these tips I learned doing all those dishes along the way.

For your pots and pans, scrape as much off as you can with a wooden spoon. The wood is not likely to harm your pans. Immersing the pan in cold water while it's hot sometimes helps loosen charred food. Use a good plastic scrubber to remove the balance. As a last resort, you can use steel wool.

After you've scraped off what you can with the wooden spoon, try pouring on what's left in the pan or oven and then heat. The remainder should flake off with the salt. If that doesn't get your pan clean, fill it half full of water and a strong detergent and boil for fifteen minutes. Let it stand for four to eight hours, depending on how tough the job. Clean it with a scrubbing pad and then a soft cloth. It should be as good as new.

Any dark deposits left in aluminum or enamel cookware can be removed by making a paste of two tablespoons cream of tartar and a little water and rubbing it on the deposits. Let it sit ten minutes and scrub. If that doesn't work, boil a big onion covered with water in the pan and that should bring the burned material to the top.

Odors aren't so difficult unless the entire house was permeated. It helps to open doors and windows. I am assuming you turned your fan on as soon as you discovered you had a problem. If you haven't cleaned your fan for a while, that really cuts down on its efficiency. You should wash the filter at least monthly and give it a thorough cleaning twice a year. It's not that tough a job. They do accumulate a fair amount of grease and dust. Follow the manufacturer's directions. You'll be surprised how much better you can solve your kitchen odor problems with a well-maintained fan. In the restaurants, we clean those huge fans at least once a month. In the first Black Angus, the exhaust vent wafted those delicious cooking odors down to the traffic signal where cars were stopped at the light. It was an accidental sales pitch and received a number of favorable comments. Wish we could have taken it with us to all our locations.

For any remaining odors, get out those old standbys—vinegar, baking soda, bread, and salt—or use a good spray throughout the house. Try putting some orange or lemon peel in your oven and cranking it up to about 325 degrees. When it gets nice and hot, turn it off and open the door for a while. You'll swear you're in an citrus grove on a sunshiny day. Put what's left of the peel through your garbage disposal to freshen up that piece of equipment. You can also rub lemon peel or slices on your cutting board to help cover up strong odors from onions an such.

About all that's left to clean is the sink. If it's light colored, fill it with warm water and add a little chlorine bleach. Wait an hour, drain, and wipe clean. If you have stubborn spots, soak a cloth with chlorine, place it directly on the stain, and leave it overnight. With a stainless-steel sink, use a nonabrasive cleaner.

Sometimes, after you've burned your meat, you'll find yourself freshening your whole kitchen. It's not all bad.

Customers nowadays are more interested in how beef is selected and prepared in restaurant kitchens. What inquiring minds need (or want) to know! Some wonder why their home-cooked steak or roast never quite measures up to what the restaurant serves. "What goes wrong?" they ask. Let me guess.

Overcooking: This produces greater shrinkage and decreases the tenderness and juiciness.

Not allowing the roast to stand after cooking: Standing allows the roast to finish cooking (about fifteen minutes). The meat will be firmer, retain more of its juices, and also be easier to carve.

Over salting the meat: Salting while cooking takes away the discretionary use of this enhancer by the people consuming the meat. Many salt without tasting which can result in over salting. We salt lightly and tell our guests so.

Failure to use a timer: A timer is very important. Get a loud one that lasts long enough to give you ample warning and USE IT. It's too easy to get distracted.

Failure to use a meat thermometer: Buy a thermometer. There's the kind you stick into the meat before it goes in the oven. They have the instant thermometer that provides you with a reading in seconds, but don't put the meat back in the oven with the thermometer in it because the plastic face will melt. They also have ones that are built right into your oven. Again, USE ONE OF THESE, in addition to the timer.

Marinating too thick a steak: A marinade only penetrates one-quarter inch into the meat. Score a diamond pattern into both sides of meat that is thicker, being careful not to cut all the way through. This will allow more meat to absorb the marinade.

Braising at too high a temperature: The higher the temperature, the greater the shrinkage and moisture loss. High temperatures tend to toughen meat since you are actually boiling the beef. Simmer—don't boil. The oven should be no higher than 325 degrees.

Broiling a cut that's too thin: Steaks less than three-quarters of an inch thick should be pan-broiled or placed on an outside grill. Too high a temperature when broiling can also cause excessive spattering and smoking.

Cooking meat in advance and reheating: This can be done, but optimum flavor and moistness is found in freshly cooked beef. It must be refrigerated until reheated for serving.

Holding cooked beef in oven too long: For optimum eating quality, hold for only an hour, loosely covered to keep it from drying out. Beef may be held safely for up to four hours as long as it's held at a temperature above 140 degrees. This is not recommended, however, because it'll become dry.

Roasting meat wrapped in aluminum foil: When roasts are cooked in foil they are braised—not roasted. This is a moist heat method. Same with baked potatoes. Common mistake.

Roasting large cuts (fourteen to sixteen pounds) at regular temperatures such as 350: Large roasts should be cooked at lower temperatures, such as 300 degrees, to ensure uniform doneness.

Not cooking beef because of fat and calories: Read Chapter 15. Start with *lean* beef, and remember, it has the same fat content and number of calories as roasted chicken without the skin. Season with herbs and spices rather than using a marinade containing oil. Trim all outside fat. Bake, broil, or roast on a grill or rack so the beef will remain above the drippings. Braise or oven broil rather than fry. Remove the drippings as they accumulate when browning beef.

Last, but certainly not least! . . .

Using "select" grade beef instead of "choice" grade: Select is tougher and a less tasty cut of beef so you're in a hole before you start. It's not worth it.

What do you do if you end up with an overcooked, dried-out piece of meat? Maybe it was a poor selection to start with, but whatever the reason, it's not wonderful the way it is. Try making hash out of it. Place it in your food processor or blender, a small amount at a time, processing it in spurts just until it's coarsely chopped. (If you don't have a processor, finely chop the meat or run it through an old-fashioned meat grinder.) Combine about two cups meat with two cups of cooked and chopped potatoes and two-thirds cup chopped onion. Add a little chopped parsley, salt, and pepper. Brown in about two teaspoons of oil ten to fifteen minutes, turning frequently. Stir in approximately two-thirds cup water, reduce heat, cover, and simmer another ten minutes, or until crisp. The last few minutes, you can make wells in the hash and drop an egg in each one, place cover on again, and cook to desired doneness (five to ten minutes). There's also the old barbecue trick discussed above. Just shred the beef, add a commercial barbecue sauce, and heat. Serve poured over hamburger buns.

Or just forget it and go out for dinner. I always enjoy going out. (My wife told me to say that.)

HEY, I'M DOUBLE-PARKED HERE—MOVE IT!

CHAPTER 17

COOKING IS A NECESSITY
KNOWING HOW IS AN ART

Of all the gin joints, in all the towns in the West, she had to walk into one of mine! Someone had me in mind when Helen was created—she's the best thing that ever happened to me.

I'm reminded of the story of a gentlemen advising a young man to: "Find one who cooks, never mind the looks." Well, I found one who cooks *and* has the looks. She can cook as if she were on the side of the angels. Most everything she knows she learned from me. Well, maybe a couple of things!

She does have one questionable habit, and let's see if I can tell this without getting into too much trouble. For years, I've called Helen "the daughter of Waste King." If I don't guard my plate with great care, she unashamedly attacks it. She's been known to go after our friends' and relatives' meals also—fork in hand. To my knowledge, she has not made any moves on a stranger yet, but I watch her carefully.

When we eat at home, Helen doesn't usually display a great appetite. It seems to me, she eats a lot less at home than when we go out, nor is she as likely to go after my plate.

One night, as I watched my evening news and fondled the remote, I noticed in the reflection of the window, my wife cooking AND EATING. After observing this for several nights, I asked, as she was ready to take another bite: "Are you eating without me?"

The quick reply was, "No, I have to sample the cooking to be sure it's just right for you!" Yeah, right! She really does the taste thing to extreme.

As some wise individual once said, "I love being married. It's so great to find that one person you get to annoy for the rest of your life."

Even with her healthy appetite, Helen manages to keep a great figure. She does this by eating a balanced diet, and she doesn't have my weakness for desserts or sweets. For that, I both pity and envy her. I always have a yearning for these creations and a special appreciation of anything chocolate. The fact that Helen is allergic to chocolate probably helps her say no. And, yes, you're right: To protect my dessert plate, I order anything I can with chocolate in it.

In 1970, after establishing our base in Washington with five stores, we moved out of state for the first time. I had a tip from a hotel supply house about a restaurant going toes up in San Diego, California. I've loved that city for a long time so proceeded to explore a deal. The building was at the edge of the city, but visible from one of those great San Diego freeways and right next door to General Dynamics. I struck another landlord arrangement, and that restaurant is still successfully operating after almost twenty-seven years.

Something more came from the out-of-state experience. The move coincided with the hiring of our future executive chef, Ray "Frenchy" Hilfiger, who brought our menu selections to a higher level. Ray just happened to be seeking a new challenge and we were there to offer it to him. In his own inimitable way, he gave us a great start in the first venture outside our own territory. It was the first of some forty-two stores in California, and I believe he was involved in the opening of every one of them, plus many more as we expanded into eighteen states. Frenchy was integral in helping us build the original Black Angus/Cattle Company Chain. He knew

In the kitchen with Helen

STU'S NEWS ALSO HONORS CHEF RAYMOND

Congratulations to **Raymond Hilfiger**, Southern Division Executive Chef! **Ray** was named "Chef of the Year" by the Chefs d'Cuisine Ass'n. of San Diego on March 31st at the Annual Chefs Ball held at the Towne and Country Hotel in San Diego. The Chefs d'Cuisine Ass'n. is a local branch of the American Culinary Federation. The Chef of the Year Award is presented each year to the outstanding member chef as selected by the nominating committee.

The qualification guidelines include proficiency in all the culinary arts, offices held, awards received and services rendered to the A.C.F.

Chef **Ray** easily satisfied those requirements, especially in service — he is a charter member of the ACF with 20 years service.

Chef **Ray** is a Certified Executive Chef of the ACF and a member of the American Academy of Chefs. He has been a college instructor of Culinary Arts and is a holder of the Careme Medal, awarded by the ACF and highly prized in the profession.

Chef **Ray** is formerly of Mulhouse, France, and is curently residing in San Diego with his wife **Irene**. He has one daughter, **Josiane**. Chef **Ray** has worked for Black Angus Restaurants for 10 years.

Executive Chef Ray Hilfiger

An article from a 1980 in-house newsletter

how to cook, but more important, he knew how to teach cooking and build morale at the same time. Every morning, Frenchy put a crazy, fun slogan on the kitchen's swinging door. We all looked forward to this daily food for thought—such as "life is dull only to dull people." It was hard not to come out with a smile. The most important thing you put on in the morning is your expression.

Today, Frenchy has a very successful consulting business in San Diego where he lives with his wife, Irene.

It's time to do something with that piece of meat you have in the refrigerator so here's some information that could help you.

CUTS OF BEEF
AND THE COOKING METHOD

It's important to choose the proper cooking method to produce flavorful, juicy beef entrees. The best method depends primarily on the tenderness of the beef cut. The function of a muscle in the live animal has a definite effect on its tenderness. Please look at the diagram on pages 184–185 as each area of the animal and the cuts of meat are discussed. The cooking methods will be considered in more detail later in this chapter.

The more a muscle is used, the tougher the meat, and the longer it has to be cooked using moist heat. Good examples are the locomotion muscles—such as shoulders and legs—which contain a greater amount of connective tissue and should be cooked at low temperatures with moisture added. This method is called *braising*. Some of the less tender cuts are the chuck, shank, brisket, and round, all of which must be covered and cooked in liquid at a low temperature—Swiss steak, pot roast, and corned beef come to mind. Don't throw in the towel, there's a lot of flavor here which easily justifies the extra time spent in cooking.

The internal movement muscles—found in the rib cage and abdominal areas—also have large, coarsely-textured muscle fibers.

229

Examples of these are the short plate or short ribs, flank steak, and skirt steak. The plate and ribs need a combination of moisture and heat to get a tenderizing effect. You can marinate the flank steak, grill it, and serve it thinly sliced for excellent eating. Skirt steaks can be grilled without marinating because of the way the thin slices are rolled and packaged in today's market.

The support muscles that have no movement—the ribs themselves and the loin (sirloin and short loin)—can be cooked with dry heat such as roasting, broiling, or frying because they have smaller and smoother muscle fibers with less connective tissue and are therefore more tender.

Some medium-tender cuts, from younger animals, can be cooked with dry heat but for a longer period at a lower temperature. Some less tender cuts can be tenderized and then roasted if you cook the beef for a much longer time using low heat. High temperatures for long periods make the meat tough, dry, and less tender. Slower cooking will break down the muscles, releasing all the flavor.

Tenderizing can be done by pounding the hell out of it with a tenderizing mallet, which you can purchase in any housewares department, or by using the side of a small plate. You can also soak it in an acidic (vinegar, wine, or lemon) marinade for at least six hours before cooking. I've included a couple of great marinades in the recipe portion of the book. As I mentioned, a marinade will only penetrate about one-fourth of an inch and, therefore, it's most effective on cuts not over a half-inch thick. It helps to use a knife to cut part way through the meat on both sides with a diagonal pattern on thicker cuts to let the marinade penetrate farther. This is called *scoring*.

Lastly, when ready to serve the finished product, always cut diagonally across the grain of the meat in thin slices (called English cut) for the most tender bites.

COOKING METHODS

You can cook beef several ways, but let's talk about the tender cuts first.

Roasting: This is cooking meat ***uncovered***, using dry heat, usually in the oven or on an enclosed grill. This works well on the prime rib, tenderloin, and top round roasts. You can also dry-roast the rump and tip roasts, but braising is preferred for those.

Flavor your meat (Johnny's Seasoning Salt and Lawry's Seasoned Pepper are favorites at our house) and brown it in a little olive oil in a heavy pan that can be transferred to the oven. After it's brown on all sides, place a rack in the pan, lay the roast on the rack fat-side up so it bastes itself, and **being careful of the steam**, add some boiling water to the bottom of the pan which will result in some wonderful juices for a brown sauce (called gravy by some). Insert a meat thermometer halfway, making sure it doesn't touch bone or fat, and pop the roast in the oven at 325 to 350 degrees for the length of time designated on the charts in this section.

Instead of browning the roast on the stove, another option is to pre-heat your oven to 450 degrees, set the meat on a rack in a pan, and place it in the oven. Bake it for fifteen minutes, then turn the temperature down to 325 degrees and cook for the remaining amount of time according to the chart, using the lower number of minutes per pound. This works best with bone-in roasts such as a standing rib.

A lot of today's ovens have a thermometer that works automatically. You insert one end into the meat and the other into the side of the oven. You set the desired temperature and put it on the *temperature probe* setting, and it will shut the oven off when it's done. A great device.

Don't remove the thermometer too early as a lot of juice will be lost from the hole it left. The meat will usually continue to cook another five degrees after removing it from the oven. Before carving, always allow your finished roast to rest for fifteen to twenty minutes, which is a good time to make the gravy (see recipe on page 303) and get the rest of the meal ready for the table.

Internal temperature of the roast should be:

> 140 degrees for rare
> 160 degrees for medium
> 170 degrees for well-done

Note: The following are based on a roast taken directly from the refrigerator.

Minutes per lb. in a 325-degree oven:

> 6 - 8 lb. rib roast w/bones, 16-20 rare, 22-24 med., 27-30 well
> 4 - 6 lb. rolled rib roast, 26-30 rare, 32-34 med., 37-40 well
> 4 - 6 lb. boneless rump, 25-30 min./lb. to desired temperature
> 3 - 4 lb. tip, 35-40 min./lb. to desired temperature
> 4 - 6 lb. top round, 25-30 min./lb. to desired temperature

Minutes per lb. in 350-degree oven:

> 4 - 6 lb. rib eye, 18-20 rare, 20-22 med., 22-24 well
> 1 1/2 lb. meat loaf, 1 1/2 hours total time

Total time in 425-degree oven:

> *Whole or half a tenderloin, 25 to 60 minutes for rare

*The technique for roasting this costly cut of beef is different because of the tenderness, lack of fat, and its long narrow shape. It should be cooked quickly at a high temperature. Use your thermometer. See recipe for "Roast Tenderloin of Beef with Madeira Sauce."

A couple of notes on roasts: If you use frozen beef, I have to tell you not to let it thaw at room temperature. It should be defrosted in the refrigerator. We do like to let our roasts and steaks sit out on a clean surface for an hour or less before cooking as we prefer our beef medium rare, and it cooks to a more even temperature when the interior of the meat is not so cold. This is not allowed in a commercial kitchen. The theory is, it takes up to two hours before harmful bacteria starts forming, and then you are adequately cooking the surface area which will kill any bad bugs. Just remember, the cooking times listed are for refrigerated meat. It takes less time for room temperature meat.

If you do elect to roast one of the less tender cuts—such as a high-quality bottom round, chuck eye, rump, or eye-of-the-round—use the basic method above, but cook in a 250- to 300-degree oven slightly longer per pound to an internal temperature of 140 to 150 degrees.

If meat is extremely lean, rub it with a vegetable oil to help keep it moist or use picks to hold two or three slices of bacon on top.

Pan-frying or pan-broiling: These terms are basically the same except more oil is used for frying; the difference lies in the fact pan-broiling needs a nonstick pan and some oil spray or spices such as those used in Cajun cooking. We really don't recommend either one for a good steak when the grill is close by, unless you're doing something like "Steak Diane," "Steak With Brandied Onions," or stir-fry (see recipes). If you do want to fry meat, do it with thin strips of beef or tenderized cuts. Cook at moderate temperature, turning the meat occasionally. Brown on both sides. Again, just before cooking, sprinkle with seasoned salt and pepper. A mixture of olive oil and butter is a nice combination for frying beef. The butter gives it a little more flavor and it browns nicely. (Only oils that can take high temperatures should be used for wok cooking—not butter.) Remove from pan immediately and serve at once.

The question of whether to season meat before cooking or after is an ongoing debate. It's my belief that seasoning before puts a lot more flavor in the meat, making the taste more subtle, the way seasonings should be. It doesn't make the meat bleed unless you put it on hours before cooking. That's an old wives' tale.

233

Cooking Time for Steaks: The best way to test a steak to your likeness is to use your finger to poke the meat. A little testing using this method will make you an expert in short order—no pun intended. There is a timetable below which includes the best cuts for broiling, but to develop your sense of touch, try this: With your right hand, take hold of the skin between your thumb and forefinger on your left hand, pinch lightly about one-half inch up, and feel the texture. This is equivalent to a rare steak. Now move up that space approximately another half inch. That's how a medium steak feels. Now move to the spot above that, about two inches into the hand and that's how a well-done steak feels. A little practice will make you an expert.

This timetable is just an approximate guide. Times will vary depending on the temperature and thickness of the meat, kind of heat source, and the equipment used.

Weight/Cut/Thickness	Inches From Heat	Time in minutes turning once Rare	Med.
1" Rib, rib eye, or top loin, 1/2 - 1 lb.	3 - 4	15	20
1 1/2" Rib, rib eye, or top loin, 1/2 - 2 lb.	4 - 5	25	30
1" Sirloin, T-bone, or porterhouse, 1 1/2 lb.	3 - 4	20	25
1 1/2" Sirloin, T-bone/porterhouse, 2 - 4 lb.	4 - 5	30	35
4 - 8 oz. Tenderloin	2 - 4	10-15	15-20
1/2" Ground beef patties, 4 oz.	3 - 4	-	12
1" Ground beef patties, 5 1/2 oz.	3 - 4	-	18

Stir-frying: This is basically the Asian version of pan-frying and a very healthful and fast way to cook. Because this method is quick-cooking, it seals in the nutrients, texture, flavor, and color of the food while keeping fat to a minimum. It's done using thin strips of beef cut diagonally across the bias of the grain, about one-eighth-inch thick, and chopping the vegetables to bite size. It helps to partially freeze the meat as it makes it much easier to slice thinly.

Marinate the beef strips while preparing the other ingredients, or you can have it all done ahead of time, storing each item in a separate bowl or baggy. Preparation is ninety percent of the job. The cooking just takes minutes, and you won't have time to do anything else once you start, so have everything else ready.

Stir-fried foods are cooked over high heat while stirring constantly. Electric woks don't get as hot as I like them, so use a good-quality, heavy wok directly on the burner. They usually come with a ring to sit the wok on since it has a rounded bottom. The burner should be on high to start. Trickle the oil down the edges or roll the wok to spread the oil. Always use an oil that can tolerate high temperatures, such as peanut, olive, or vegetable. Test by dropping a piece of vegetable in the oil. If it sizzles, it's ready. You can turn it down slightly when you start to keep from burning, but this type of cooking requires high heat.

Add your stir-fry seasonings first—garlic, red pepper, ginger, onions—so they'll release their flavor, but only for fifteen to thirty seconds to avoid scorching. When stir-frying, you must keep everything moving at all times using a wooden spatula.

Do the vegetables next. They should be added in the order of the time it takes to cook each one. For example, broccoli, carrots, celery, onions, and such take longer to cook than pea pods, cabbage, water chestnuts, or bean sprouts. Several stir-fry recipes can be found in the recipe section and the ingredients should be cooked in the order listed. When all the vegetables are al dente, remove them from the pan and keep them warm.

Now comes the meat. You will probably need to add more oil. Put in no more than one-third pound of meat at a time to ensure that the wok remains hot. Adding too much food at once cools it down rapidly and the food is steamed instead. Combine the meat, vegetables, and whatever sauces the recipe calls for and serve immediately over rice or Chinese noodles. Add fragile ingredients, such as tomatoes, tofu, green onion tops, orange sections, and so forth, after all ingredients have been combined.

If you're watching your fat, use an oil spray, do a brief stir-fry and then add a small amount of beef or chicken broth. Cover briefly, then remove cover and stir until liquid is gone. Then proceed with the sauce. Remember that soy is very salty, so taste before lifting that salt shaker.

Broiling: This means to cook by direct overhead heat in an oven. It's a low-fat method of cooking steaks and ground beef patties. Less tender cuts such as flank or top round should be marinated before broiling. We prefer the grill over broiling.

Remove excess fat to avoid fire flare-ups when broiling. Score the edges to prevent the meat curling up. You can brush your lean steaks with oil or butter to brown them more. Preheat the broiler so it's good and hot when you place the steak under it. If you don't, the meat will steam instead of broil. You won't like what that does to your meat.

Season and place the meat on the broiler pan rack (if you spray with a little oil first, clean-up will be a lot easier). The meat should be one to two inches thick, and the distance from the heat depends upon that thickness. Move it farther away if the meat is thicker (see chart on page 234). When nice and brown, turn and broil the other side. Serve immediately.

Braising: This method uses moist heat at lower temperatures on less tender cuts of meat. Pot roasting is a common term when braising large cuts. This method is best for arm roasts and steaks, blade roasts and steaks, boneless chuck pot roasts (one of our favorites) and steaks, short ribs and shanks, round steaks, rump roasts, and so forth.

Season all sides of the meat and brown over medium heat in a heavy fry pan or Dutch oven in a small amount of oil. Add liquid (water, wine, beef broth, vegetable juice, canned tomatoes, or whatever the recipe calls for). Cover and simmer slowly at a low temperature, either on the stove burner or in a moderate, 325-degree oven until beef is fork tender. See cooking time chart that follows. Check periodically to be sure there's plenty of liquid.

Add vegetables toward the end of the cooking time. After removing the meat and vegetables, skim as much fat off the surface as possible. If you don't want to add calories, just use the liquid au jus—its natural state. After the meat and vegetables have been removed, you can boil the juices down so they're more concentrated, then season to taste. If you prefer a thicker texture or want to extend it for a larger group, see the brown sauce (gravy) recipe.

Approximate Total Cooking Time:

	Hours
3 - 5 lb. blade pot roast	2 to 2 1/2
3 - 5 lb. arm pot roast or boneless chuck roast	2 1/2 to 3 1/2
2x2x4" short ribs or ox joints	1 1/2 to 2 1/2
1 1/2 - 2 lb. flank steak	1 1/2 to 2 1/2
3/4" - 1" thick round steak	1 to 1 1/2

Cooking in Liquid: This is moist heat cooking when the meat is covered with liquid such as corned brisket, short ribs, stew meat, and so forth.

You usually coat the beef with seasoned flour (except corned brisket) and then brown in a small amount of oil. Always pour off excess fat before proceeding with the recipe. Cover beef completely with liquid (type can vary as in braising) to ensure uniform cooking. Cover the pot tightly, bring to a boil, then reduce heat and simmer on the stovetop or in the oven until fork tender.

Approximate Total Cooking Time:

	Hours
4 - 6 lb. fresh or corned brisket	3 1/2 to 4 1/2
3/4 - 1 1/2lb. cross-cut shank	2 1/2 to 3
Beef stew	2 to 3

Microwaved Beef: I don't recommend this method. It's okay to use a medium power to reheat braised beef as leftovers, but it just doesn't do justice to a good piece of beef.

IT DOESN'T GET ANY BETTER THAN THIS!

Two-inch, well-aged, prime porterhouse steaks on the grill cooking over mesquite coals, martinis from the bottle of Bombay Sapphire gin I keep in the freezer, a little Beethoven in the background, and the company of good friends—I plan to be buried in a place like that. Ben Franklin said something like: "Beef is sure proof that God loves us and wants us to be happy." I confess I took some liberties with that quote—maybe it was wine, but I'll take either one.

Barbecue is the slow cooking of beef or pork over hot smoke from hickory wood—at least that's what they'll tell you in many Southern states. What we do in our backyards is mostly *grilling*. So let's review some things for this outdoor adventure.

First, I'm going to assume you have an outdoor grill. If you don't, get one! The prices can run from twenty dollars to a thousand and more. The cheaper grills are charcoal fueled, but that's all right, just a little more work. Many grills are gas-fired and start around two hundred dollars. Be sure you get the appropriate one for natural gas or propane. There's a difference.

Even if you buy the less expensive ones, be sure you have a cover so you can roast, bake, and smoke foods. The better ones have different settings for searing, broiling, roasting, and smoking. You can actually move the heating element on some so it's in different positions in relation to the food. This eliminates splattering, flare-ups, and smoking. Other great features to look for: energy efficiency, a side burner, a warming oven, surrounding work space to set things on, either an adjustable cooking rack (should move four to six inches) or control of flame height, adjustable cover ventilation, ease of cleaning (bottoms drop down on some), and a rotisserie. Of course, the cost goes up with the added benefits.

Some new stove-top grills work fairly well, if any sissies out there don't like braving the elements. They have a ring of water under the grill that catches the drips so there's hardly any smoke.

These work better with gas stoves; however, they can be used with electric. Some manufacturers make indoor grills and rotisseries for your stove top that plug in as an alternative to your burners. For our motor home, we recently purchased a smaller electric grill with a cover and rotisserie. The heating element and grill are designed so grease doesn't spatter; consequently, there's no smoke, so it can be used indoors.

The most energy-efficient grill uses the least amount of BTUs to get the cooking done. A British Thermal Unit (BTU) is a standard unit of energy equal to the heat required to raise a pound of water one degree Fahrenheit. Compare the BTU output or wattage between models with the *same size* cooking surface. This will tell you which one uses the most energy. Of the three grill types, gas and electric are comparable in efficiency; charcoal is the least efficient and most polluting. Also, most people start it with lighter fluid which is a petroleum distillate that emits volatile organic compounds, further contributing to smog. Some areas of California have banned lighter fluids unless the label states the product meets the "South Coast Air Quality Management District standards." Instead, use a charcoal chimney (found in places that sell charcoal), an electric starter, or just balled-up newspaper and some twigs. And NEVER add lighter fluid to a fire that has already started! Electric grills are the least polluting, although many feel they don't give that wonderful flavor to the meat, but I'll discuss this later. Another source of pollution is the smoke from the fat drippings falling into the fire.

This brings us to the two methods of cooking—direct and indirect. With direct, food is placed on the grid directly above the coals; this is for beef which cooks in a relatively short time—steaks, burgers, and kabobs. Trim visible fat from the exterior of your steaks which helps keep down flare-ups. The indirect method cooks food for a longer period and more slowly by reflective heat, similar to an oven. Separate the coals, put an aluminum-foil drip pan in between the coals, place your meat over the drip pan, close the cover, and follow the recipe for times and temperature. This method greatly reduces flare-ups.

You'll need some tools with long handles, a fireproof mitt, skewers, a grill basket for cooking smaller items, and a stiff wire brush for cleaning the grill. Long-handled tongs are best for turning steaks so you don't puncture the meat and let the juices out. Have a spray bottle handy for flare-ups, or just close the lid if you have one.

Cooking on rotisseries is really hot in this country. Many restaurants have a mouth-watering roast or bird on a spit for you to savor as you enter or pass by en route to your table. It's a great marketing tool and results in delicious-tasting meat. Cooking in this manner goes way back, before the Neanderthals, when someone figured out that meat over a fire tasted better than the steak tartare less intelligent neighbors were eating. When meat is electrically rotating on a spit, the fat and juices are continuously basting the meat, making it very moist. It's my favorite way to cook ribs, roasts, and whole chickens.

We had a large grill in our party barn at the ranch which served five hundred people at one setting. Sarah Foster, our ranch chef (see back of book jacket), had given up her lucrative job as chef of Stuart's at Shilshole, my grand experiment in seafood. I built it using Arnie Bystrom as architect and Stephen Chase as interior designer—nothing but the best. It was a beautiful structure on the waterfront in Seattle's Ballard district. Saga sold it at a nice profit and informed me after the fact. Sarah is the only association I have left from that adventure. She and her husband, Fast Eddy, wanted to raise a family in the country. That was to our benefit, because she went to work for us at the ranch. Sarah skewered whole top sirloin roasts called *steak ready* (if sliced, they would be sirloin steaks) and slowly roasted them, turning frequently, over red oak we imported from a guy called Woody Woodpecker in California. That meat was incredible! Add Sarah's perfected baked beans (see recipe section), a baked potato with all

Getting ready for a crowd at the party barn

the trimmings, two salads—fruit and tossed—garlic bread hot off the grill, corn on the cob, and some strawberry shortcake, and you'd be hard pressed to beat it. Many of you enjoyed the hospitality in the big party barn and will vouch for this. As of this writing, she's still making a lot of folks happy with her cooking at the barn.

If you want to add more flavor to your meat, try one of the following:

1. Experiment with different woods that lend perfume to the smoke. (Don't try to use woods indoors!) One of the most common is mesquite which gives a rich, woody, and clean flavor. Because it's grown in arid climates, mesquite retains a lot of moisture so gives off a heavy smoke when burned. The packaged mesquite chunks are usually heat dried so they last longer. Mesquite burns hot and is best with beef and other robust foods. Hickory is probably the next most common and works well with beef, ribs, and pork. Alder emits a more delicate smoke and is wonderful with fish. Fruitwood prunings, such as apple, elder, and grapevine give off a wonderful fruity flavor. Some experts swear they can even tell if it's a Riesling or Gewurztraminer wood the meat has been cooked with. I doubt that. At any rate, as an alternative, you can soak wood *chips* and toss them on the coals after they get going. If using gas or electric, put the wet chips in a small metal container (or make one out of heavy-duty foil) and set it on a small portion of the heating element during the cooking process. This does pass on some flavor.

2. Tie herbs together in bundles and nestle next to the meat on the grill, especially if using the indirect method. Soak all herbs in water for half an hour before putting them on the fire so they'll smolder, not burn. Try rosemary, thyme, basil, dill, and oregano.

3. Toss lemon, lime, or orange rinds on the coals. For beef, try garlic cloves, onion sections, or fennel slices. Sweet spices, such as cinnamon sticks, cloves, whole nutmeg, or the like, are great for Indian and Middle Eastern dishes.

4. Try rubs with different combinations of thyme, minced garlic, parsley, sage, rosemary, dry mustard, paprika, basil, onion powder, curry, chili powder, and so on—whatever flavors your taste buds prefer. It's best if you rub the meat with these at least a half hour before cooking.

5. Marinate your meat. Hundreds of recipes can be found for good marinades. Besides adding flavor, the acid in the ingredients tenderize the meat as mentioned earlier in this chapter. The ratio of the oil to the acidic item you're using—wine, vinegar, or citrus juice—varies depending on the type of food. For beef, you'll want about twice as much of one of these to the oil (one cup wine to a half cup oil).

6. Try thin jams diluted with orange or pineapple juice, or apricot jam mixed with spicy mustard. Marinades with a high sugar content should be applied the last fifteen to twenty minutes because they'll char easily.

7. If you want that grilled flavor but don't want to spend a lot of time outside, you can sear the roast or whatever you're cooking on the grill, then bring it indoors and finish it in the oven. Or you can reverse this and start it indoors, but finish it on the grill.

Remember, never put the cooked meat on the same platter you took the raw meat out to the grill with unless you've thoroughly washed it, and don't reuse utensils that were in contact with the raw meat.

If using coals, allow at least twenty minutes to get them hot. Eighty percent of the coals should be ash white and glowing. Hot fires have a low flame and red, glowing coals; a medium fire has a red glow but no flame; and with a low fire, the coals are covered with gray-white ash and there is no red glow.

COOKING TIMES AND METHODS

Weight/ Thickness	Method	Heat	Time
Steaks, 1" thick	direct	medium	4 to 6 minutes per side for rare
Hamburger	direct	medium	4 minutes per side.
2 - 3 lb. roast	indirect	medium	45 - 60 minutes*
4 lb. rib roast	indirect	medium	1 - 2 1/4 hours*
Kabobs on coals	direct	medium	15 - 20 minutes**
Kabobs on gas	indirect	medium	15 - 20 minutes**

* use an instant-read thermometer
**turning and basting as they cook

Good luck, and don't forget the apron. It doesn't need one of those stupid sayings on it, but, who knows, you might cheer up someone's day. Enjoy the fragrance of the smoke and of that beef grilling. Someone should invent a perfume that duplicates that beautiful aroma.

CHAPTER 18

BEEF AND
THE NATURAL PARTNERS

This chapter is short because it really isn't about beef. It's about the stuff you see hanging around with it. And you can't have beef without some knowledge and appreciation for these natural partners, specifically potatoes and garlic bread

THE MAGIC OF GARLIC

That all-important, magical garlic clove—is it a medicine, a food, or just something to ward off vampires?

You'll notice I've had a lot of love affairs, speaking of food of course, and one of them is with garlic. I'm aware some cooks might not care for garlic, so if you prefer, leave it out. Try using shallots instead. If you do, you'll miss the medicinal benefits some say result from eating garlic regularly. Supposedly, it can reduce blood pressure and lower cholesterol levels.

Instead of putting a pat of butter or margarine on bread, use olive oil laced with garlic as a tasty spread. This will replace saturated with monounsaturated fat, if you have a cholesterol problem.

How about this one from Pennsylvania State University? First they transplanted human colon cancer cells in mice, then some of the mice were treated with a chemical found in processed garlic. The others got a placebo. The tumors in mice getting the garlic shrank by sixty percent; the tumors in the others continued to grow. Of course, we're talking of mice—not men.

Here's another story from the Pasteur Institute in France. Garlic eaters tested there reported less anxiety and irritability with a greater sense of well-being, and the institute claimed it was because of serotonin—a chemical known as the "calming chemical"—found in garlic. Once again, more research is probably needed, but that's not my job—I just report it. Besides, I don't think anyone really has proved any of this conclusively.

In the early days of the Black Angus chain, I had more requests for the secret of our ranch garlic bread than anything else. I always said, "Sorry, I can't let you have it." If they persisted and pleaded, I told them: "Okay, I'll give it to you, but then I'll have to kill you." Well, now it can be told. After all, you bought the book. You'll find my *secret* in the recipe section under "Original Ranch Bread" on page 301. Actually, the real secret to our recipe was that we could get our bread so fresh every day. That was because of the large volume we did. How fresh was it? It was *sooooo* fresh we had to cut it with a *heated* serrated knife.

Do you have to go to France to get French bread?

YESTERDAY . . . WHEN I WAS YOUNG

The trick in driving a Sherman thirty-ton tank is to make a smooth turn. You steer with levers and make turns by holding back or stopping one track while the opposite side spins around. Kind of a herky-jerky pirouette.

Normally, no problem; however, when we went through Paris, the population came out in force. Everyone waved white hankies, as if surrendering with joy, and in their enthusiasm to greet us, they narrowed the road considerably. Making a turn in that happy mass of humanity was spooky. I feared running over their toes, but don't believe I ever did.

It was true wherever we went. The joy of the people in "Mudville," as we called the small, rain-soaked towns, seemed even more pronounced the closer we moved toward Germany. A warning order came down from Patton's headquarters not to take anything into our vehicles that people gave us along our route. I don't know if it was a rumor or a fact, but supposedly a soldier had done exactly that and the little "gift" blew up, killing everyone inside the tank. We had to watch our driving, and now we also had to watch the people crowding in on us as we passed by.

In one small town they seemed especially happy to see us, and an attractive lady with a beautiful smile approached the tank. It was a lovely fall day and all was right with the world. I tried to match her smile as she handed me a loaf of bread. I just couldn't see myself throwing the bread back at her or dropping it like a hot potato. It felt warm and soft like it was freshly baked but, believe me, I squeezed all over that loaf before taking it inside. At that moment, the world made little sense. Even though I had to share it with my tank mates, it did serve as dinner, and try as I might, I've never been able to duplicate that savory loaf of French bread. At least I learned how special it was to have a loaf fresh out of the oven.

When we first moved into California's Bay Area, the customers said we had to serve San Francisco sourdough bread. Since I always listen to customers, we switched to that famous bread. However, patrons who knew us from our other locations came into the Bay Area stores and gave us a lot of flack over the missing ranch bread. We decided to serve both and that became a real pain in the rear. After that, I gave a lot more thought to requests before making changes the crew would have to live with.

The original ranch bread was made on a large, rotating toaster, sort of a waterwheel effect. It was kind of fascinating to watch this flow of bread slowly moving on this rack. The finished pieces were

A typical Sherman tank moving through "Mudville."

placed in a warming drawer and the food servers would take them out and place them on the plates. Naturally, some pieces stayed in too long and dried out. Then there were times when the machine couldn't keep up with the crowd. In general, it was not the most efficient system. I hate to tell you how many bread-tasting sessions we had just trying to simplify the process, and in the end we changed to a basket of rolls.

There's a modern version of garlic bread offered in the restaurants as an extra option. This is a more cheesy bread and the recipe is included for those who can't resist it and want to try it at home. It's called "Garlic/Cheese Bread" on page 301. You can make this spread and keep it in the refrigerator, then use it as needed at meal time. Just spread it on as much bread as you need for the meal, then pop it into your toaster oven.

Prepared properly, garlic can add a wonderful flavor, enhance the taste of beef, bread, and many other foods, and not leave you with unpleasant breath. Cooking it reduces garlic's odorous effect. Buy a good, self-cleaning garlic press, and after pressing the garlic, sprinkle it with salt (sea salt if you have it). If you don't have a press, the best way to mince it is by hand with a sharp, heavy chef's knife. Before you start chopping, use the side of the knife to crush the cloves.

When sautéing, cook the garlic very slowly over low heat so you don't get it too dark as this makes it bitter. Try roasting it to make it more mellow. After removing most of the outer husks on the bulb, slice off the top of the cluster. We place ours in the toaster oven, set it to 300 degrees, and plug it in outside or in the garage so the garlic odor doesn't overpower the house. After an hour or so, when it starts to brown, remove it, let it cool, and squeeze each clove out of its casing. Use the paste with a Montrachet cheese on toast points and you've got a delicious hors d'oeuvre. The roasted cloves will store in the refrigerator for weeks. I can tell you, it doesn't have to reduce your circle of friends.

We frequently have a "dry" cocktail hour at our house, and to get our requirement of garlic, we fix a drink as follows: Put one large clove of garlic, a sprig of parsley, and a small amount of V-8 juice into a blender and run it for a minute or so. Then slowly add the rest of the 12-ounce can of V-8 juice. Mix and pour into two glasses over ice. Very refreshing, and supposedly, the parsley sprig helps cut down the garlic breath.

Hummus is another great and healthy way to get your garlic and is easy to prepare. See the recipe section, page 304. If you're watching fat grams and calories, the hummus is a good spread on corn or rice cakes.

I read somewhere, "There is no such thing as too much sex or too much garlic." Garlic is said to keep caterpillars and snails away from your garden. We used to feed it to our cattle to get rid of warts and it worked. I know this use doesn't do anything for your appetite, but maybe garlic truly is the nectar of the gods?

THE LOFTY POTATO

It's not how you say it—some say po-tay-to, some say po-tah-to—or even spelling—potato (the correct way) or potatoe (the Dan Quayle way)—but it's how you dress it up to be the best accompaniment to prime rib or a New York steak. That's what counts. It's the lofty potato. A diet food? Yes. A pigging-out food? Yes. Put a little nonfat yogurt or creamed cottage cheese on it and it's a great diet dish. Put some melted butter, sour cream, and bacon bits on it and you're cruising to the Big and Tall Shop next time you go shopping. A recent report claims one restaurant's stuffed baked potato had 1120 calories, with 79 fat grams. Wow! Go ahead and enjoy your favorite toppings in moderation a couple times a month; there'll be no harm done, but don't overdo it. I asked my mother at eighty-nine what her secret to a long life was, and her immediate answer was "Moderation." She kept her figure but also enjoyed good food.

One potato, two potato. . . . Potatoes originated in South America and were cultivated by the Incas as early as 3000 B.C. Potatoes are placed in categories by age. The *new potato* is an immature one, usually on the small side, and it goes to market directly from the farmer's field. New potatoes can be red or white but both have a high water content so they cook rapidly. These small potatoes are so sweet all you need to do is slice and steam, or cook whole with the skins left on.

The restaurants deal with potatoes of all sizes, ages, and shapes, but mostly they serve the *Long Russet*. This can weigh up to sixteen ounces, although that's a little big for the plate. They're the leading variety and are used primarily for bakers. Approximately thirty-five billion pounds of potatoes are harvested in the United States, with Idaho raising one-third of those and Washington one-fifth. The Northwest-grown potatoes are without peers. We featured the famous Idaho potato on the first menus. However, Washington started raising great spuds, too, and we had ten stores in Washington, with only one store in Idaho. Needless to say, we changed the terminology on our menus and that stopped the remarks we were getting. There will always be a few people out there searching for what's wrong instead of enjoying what's there.

The potato is by far the largest-selling vegetable, although they're more like a starch than a vegetable. The magic is in how to fix and dress them up. A recipe we got many requests for in the early days was the "Potatoes Au Gratin" which you'll find on page 302.

Here's a few potato pointers I've learned over the years when buying or preparing them:

1. Look for spuds without blemishes or soft spots. They should be firm, smooth, and clean. Skip the ones with sprouts unless you plan on starting your garden, they've been there too long. If it happens at home, just pick them off as they develop. The potato will keep longer.

2. Avoid ones with a slightly green color. This means they've been exposed to light too long and could taste bitter. There are also claims that the green potato is a carcinogenic but I'm sure more research is probably needed.

3. When you get them home, store them in a cool, dark spot. Do not refrigerate or store them at less than forty degrees.

4. Select bakers of similar size so they'll cook evenly—same length of time at the same temperature.

5. Scrub your potatoes with a vegetable brush before preparing if you'll be leaving the skins on.

6. For great baked potatoes, rub them with a little butter or oil, prick with a fork or stab with a small knife (this prevents them from exploding in the oven—a real mess to clean up) and bake for an hour in a conventional oven at 350 to 375 degrees. Eat immediately as a baked potato loses sixty percent of its Vitamin C if left to stand for an hour after cooking, but only twenty percent if eaten shortly after.

7. Microwaved baked potatoes are mushy inside with soft skins, but if you're in a big hurry, rub with butter, prick, microwave for two minutes, turn and microwave two more minutes (increase this time for a larger amount of potatoes), and then finish by baking the conventional way at 375 degrees for twenty minutes to half an hour. Much better than straight microwave. From experience, I don't believe beef or potatoes belong in a microwave. That equipment is great for heating your coffee or drying your wet tennis shoes. Okay, okay! I know there are many other good uses: sweet potatoes, for example, are a different story. Their skin is soft and not usually eaten, and they have a lower water content so they do fine in the microwave, as do most vegetables.

8. Another way to speed up the baking is to stick a large nail (a clean one, of course), or similar metal rod, in the middle of each potato and place in the conventional oven (NOT IN THE MICROWAVE). They'll cook much faster.

9. For potato salads or stews, select a waxy style such as the round reds.

10. If you're watching calories, don't fry potatoes—bake them. Cut in French-fry shape or slice thin. Spray a cookie sheet with oil and place potatoes on it in a single layer. Melt a little butter and lightly baste fries. You can use a vegetable oil or a mixture of both butter and oil. Bake in a 400-degree oven for fifteen minutes. Turn, baste the other side, and bake another fifteen minutes or until golden. Sprinkle with salt and serve immediately. This really uses very little butter or oil.

11. Last and most important, French fries got their start in *France*! Another little gem of information from me!

CHAPTER 19

DO UNTO OTHERS, THEN CUT OUT!

The great drama was unfolding. The passing of a 1.25 billion-dollar company, a corporation on the New York Stock Exchange, and the home of sixty thousand people was about to take place. A trail of bad judgment to **try and fix what ain't broke**, started a long, slow slide into oblivion. I know this sounds heavy and it's painful to review, but what the actions of so few did to so many should be reviewed. Let the chips fall where they may.

How did it happen and where did it start? All the actors in this tragedy probably have a different version—here's mine.

As Stuart Anderson's Restaurants approached the opening of the one hundredth store—and I attended one of the zillion corporate meetings—something was bothering me. I peered out over the beautiful campus, heard the faint songs of the birds, watched the shadows spread over the hills, listened to a guy named Paul snore, and wondered, "What am I doing here?" While some executive from the Business and Industry Division, with nothing in common with the Stuart Anderson chain, gave a lengthy and detailed report, creating the big yawn around the room in the process, I decided I really didn't need this! I had been there for eight hours with our leader, Charlie, doing most of the talking. Spend a day in a Charlie meeting and you'd swear two weeks had gone by. I could be looking for speaking engagements or drumming up media interviews in search of publicity, working the cattle at the ranch, increasing the irrigation, visiting the people in the stores, or just about anything else I could think of. This was all a monumental waste of time, and time is one thing that can't be retrieved.

Later that day, I told Jim Morrell I would like to move out of operations as president and become chairman. This way I could still be the *wheel*, a figurehead, to help with the opening of new stores and continue the TV advertising. He discussed it with Charlie who enthusiastically went along with the suggestion. That cut through my ego like a knife. I had expected, "Oh! You can't do that now. We need you!" What I got was, "Okay, when do you want it to be effective?" It later occurred to me that Charlie was happy to be in charge of the division that had the highest profit and the greatest growth potential in the company. Now I was a little sorry I had acted so fast. Was this sudden move on my part going to trigger such actions as moving the head offices from Seattle to the Bay Area? It happened. Did I start the end of an era for me and maybe other key executives? Yes.

YESTERDAY . . . WHEN I WAS YOUNG

I mine some more memories!

All things, good or bad, have to come to an end sometime, and my service years were about to do just that. Early winter in Germany was very wet in 1944 —it was either snowing or raining, and those cold days were getting shorter. In fact, that winter set a record for cold temperatures and snowfall. Ask any man who was there.

The enemy was always close now. In the still of the night we could hear the German tanks moving. We could tell because the tanks' tracks made a squeaking sound but the power units were very quiet. Our Sherman tanks were faster but much noisier, and we had a higher silhouette. Also, we mounted 75mm guns while they had those fearsome 88s. Believe me, we had justification for being more than a little nervous listening to those screechy sounds that night. They didn't seem to be either coming or going—just running somewhere off to the side of us, as best we could tell—so eventually we fell asleep.

Where and how to sleep each night was always a difficult problem. Usually we pitched a tent, but sometimes a handy building would suffice if it were close to our armored home on tracks. One night we parked near a dairy barn with a great hay loft to sleep in. I don't know, but maybe one hundred cows were in their stalls for the night. That's one of the world's most pleasant smells to me— wet cow mingled with new-mown hay. Even more vivid was the subtle noise of all those cows chewing their cud. I can't think of a more satisfying sound—maybe not to you, but for me. It's like a symphony played by a large orchestra of contented cows. Those sounds that night drowned out the two-part snores and fart harmony of my mates and placed the war in a far-off place. I wish I could have said to the farmer, "Bless this barn!" but in Germany during the war the farms and villages appeared deserted and I never saw anyone to say hello or thank you to.

There were those occasions when we had to sleep in our tanks— ready to move. I worked out a system that I'm sure other drivers before me had figured out. I'd wedge my helmet between the gun mount and the side of the tank, then tie the strap under my chin, and that would hold my head up. The next move was to place my booted feet on the still-warm engine mount, close the hatch and go off to dreamland and a better world.

But whoa . . .

The feet didn't stay there and I'd wake up with my boots in an inch of cold water which had leaked through the hatch and clear through the boots to my toes. After a few nights like that and the damp, chilly days, I had a hard time walking or even standing when I got out of the tank. I was taken to the front-line aid station where they had to cut my boots off and I saw big black feet. Ugly! I was placed on a stretcher and taken to an ambulance with three others who had feet as colorful as mine or worse. We were driven to a field hospital and carried in on the stretchers. I felt fine and told the guys carrying me that I could walk to that tent. One big, tough corporal turned and growled, "Buddy, if you tried walking on those feet you'd fall on your f_ _ _ ing face." Now I was scared. They carried me through the whole medical chain and on into Christmas in an English hospital. I had mixed feelings—half happiness and half joy. My thoughts were with my comrades near the front in that cold weather, but I loved my warm bed. I was discharged in a few months and I didn't lose one toe.

My war was at an end.

And forty years later, I was on the sideline watching another era end. In hindsight, I was wrong not to designate an heir to my position from within the Stuart Anderson chain. If you recalled back in earlier days I felt I had won the issue of succession with Charlie. Wrong! You're going to need a score card for what Charlie did with my successors—the first two didn't have any restaurant management experience. First came Ralph Pica, a Saga man. He was selected by Charlie and Jim as the new president of Stuart Anderson's Restaurants, and I approved. Ralph said he wasn't a restaurant man—he was a people person. Well, he was half right anyway. In hindsight, he was not the man for the job. I knew Ralph through Charlie's meetings and had fun kidding around with him. There was one thing about Ralph I hadn't realized—he had a temper. He would blow up at the Black Angus executive meetings, and he totally lost it with me at one of our restaurant openings. I was stunned and things were never the same—no more yucks. In a little more than a year, he was gone. His temper wasn't the only reason for his short term of office; the morale was slipping and the business just wasn't improving.

After Ralph came Fedele Bauccio, one more Saga executive, but he wasn't given a chance. Here we go again—Charlie made another move in less than a year. As a result of an acquisition of a small group of restaurants, he brought in one of the owners, Larry Mindel, to be in charge of Stuart Anderson's Restaurants—now it was the chain that didn't have a chance. He was a restaurateur, but this man was in way over his head going from a few restaurants to a one hundred and twenty-unit chain. It wasn't that he didn't

Changing of the guard—me and Ralph Pica from Saga

Left to right, Jim Morrell, me, and Charlie Lynch

Tom Lee and Fedele Bauccio, with yours truly

know, it was more that he knew so much that ain't so. Our new Mira Mesa restaurant outside San Diego, California, was within a couple of weeks of opening when Larry came aboard. Guess what? He too was **trying to fix what wasn't broke**! He spent over a quarter of a million dollars tearing up the booths, replacing them with tables and chairs, and remodeling the kitchen to install a rotisserie cooking display. He delayed the opening for more than a month and brought in a new menu. Hold onto the book—you won't believe this one!

Chickens! He had more ways of preparing chicken than Colonel Sanders of Kentucky Fried Chicken fame ever thought of, and more seafood items than Skipper's. Then, to add insult to injury, he added fennel sausages and—here it is—**rabbit.** Honestly, rabbit was one of Larry's new big feature items. Thumper didn't belong on a rancher's steak house menu.

From what I heard afterwards, Larry didn't show much respect for the people who built the Black Angus either. The morale fell at Mira Mesa and eventually throughout the whole chain. As the new menu made its way across the country, the customer count started a free-fall, followed by the profit. What did people go to the Black Angus for? A steak, of course. Charlie and Larry, with their double egos, felt that steak houses were a dying breed. What a market they missed!

The Outback Steak Houses, a very direct competitor (with 341 outlets and a net income of fifty-four million at the end of 1995), started in **1987**, one year after Charlie's sale of Saga. It's been a bull market for steak eateries in the last decade. Let me give you some examples of 1995 stock increases for competitors of Stuart Anderson Restaurants: Logan Roadhouse's stock gained three hundred and eighteen percent; Longhorn Steaks with seventy-four restaurants and expanding fast, up a hundred and nine percent; Lone Star Steak House and Saloon, which operates one hundred and seventy-five restaurants, up ninety-two percent; Outback Steak House, up fifty-three percent. That was **our** market. There is also

261

Morton's and Ruth's Chris Steak Houses, both in a higher price bracket but on the move.

Look at the listing of the restaurant chains on the next page—not one of the new steak houses, the darlings of Wall Street, were listed then. They were all getting started around the time Black Angus was going to chicken, seafood, and rabbit. All seem to be doing great and I wish them well (well okay, not too well, but well). The Stuart Anderson Restaurants have also started an ambitious expansion program into such new markets as Salt Lake City and Las Vegas, as well as in established markets such as Phoenix and Minneapolis.

There were two surveys taken on the Stuart Anderson chain just slightly before and during the time of these changes. One was polled by Bill Laughlin, one of the Saga founders, and you can imagine how thrilled we were to see Willy come around with his notebook in hand. He spent time (and I understand his own money) to rate the quality of the food, service, and customer satisfaction. He found them all wanting.

The second survey, conducted around the same time, was by the respected *Restaurants and Institutions* magazine. They presented their annual "America's Choice in Restaurant Chains Award" to the chain voted the best. Seventy-four chains were ranked through a procedure developed by the magazine in conjunction with National Family Opinion, Inc., of Toledo, Ohio. Like with most awards, it's a special honor to receive the one the general public has voted on. The Stuart Anderson chain was voted **Number One** four out of the five years from 1981 to 1985. The chain has received that honor since then, including this past year, but the exhibit I'm referring to below is important to my point.

What I want to ask the Saga founders, especially Willy and then Charlie, is:

"What is it about being voted Number One across the country that you don't understand?"

RESTAURANTS & INSTITUTIONS

STUART ANDERSON'S REGAINS
TOP SPOT AMONG AMERICA'S
FULL-SERVICE RESTAURANTS

After Benihana nudged it from first last
year, Stuart Anderson's returns as the most
popular full-service restaurant. Fuddruck-
ers, Furr's and Golden Corral broke into the
top 10.

Chain	'86	'85
Stuart Anderson's Cattle Co.	1	2
Benihana of Tokyo	2	1
TGI Friday's	3	3
Red Lobster	4	5
Fuddruckers	5	—
Furr's Cafeterias	5*	—
Bennigan's	7	6
Morrison's Cafeterias	8	11
Steak & Ale	8*	4
Golden Corral	10	—
Chi-Chi's	11	9
Bob Evan's	12	19
Shoney's	12*	—
Victoria Station	14	7
Swensen's	15	10
Pizza Hut	16	17
Friendly	16*	14
Western Sizzlin'	18	13
Houlihan's	19	—
Po Folks	20	—
Pizza Inn	21	22
Perkins	22	16
Godfather's Pizza	23	21
Mr. Steak	24	18
Ponderosa	25	25
Sizzler Family Steakhouse	26	15
Bonanza	27	20
Big Boy	28	24
International House of Pancakes	28*	26
Denny's	30	27
Country Kitchen	31	23
Shakey's	32	28
Howard Johnson	33	29

*Tie
© 1986 *Restaurants & Institutions*, a Cahners publication.

■ DINNER HOUSES

Stuart Anderson's Emerges Again as America's Favorite

Stuart Anderson's climbed back into the top spot among all full-service restaurant chains in *R&I*'s Choice in Chains survey for the fourth time in the past five years. Five other dinner house concepts also ranked in the top 10.

In fact, the four most popular restaurant chains are dinner houses. Behind No. 1 Stuart Anderson's are Benihana of Tokyo, which was last year's champion, TGI Friday's and Red Lobster. Bennigan's (No. 8) and Steak & Ale (No. 10) also make the top 10.

Chain Sizzles with the Singles, the Spenders

The things that most attract Americans to restaurants—quality of food, service and cleanliness—are the areas where Stuart Anderson's scored higher than any other dinner house chain in *R&I*'s exclusive Choice in Chains survey.

Charlie, who seemed overly concerned about showing a rise in quarterly profits as compared to the same period the previous year, was in trouble and realized his string of successes was coming to an end. Thinking back now, most involved observers felt a strong contributing factor to the demise of the Saga Corporation were the almost unreal, overzealous moves Charlie made to maintain company growth. That and the fact that the restaurant business is a people business and Charlie was more an organization person. With the changing climate in Black Angus and their other restaurants, Saga profits started falling. Charlie reacted by purchasing more restaurant companies. In Saga's name, he purchased a Texas chicken chain for 57.5 million dollars—an amazing price for a good but medium-sized chain call Grandy's. Two talented entrepreneurs did a good job building the chain and now they were about to do an even better job on Charlie.

The sale went through without one of us long-time restaurateurs being consulted about any aspect of this transaction. The top five vice presidents of the Black Angus executive committee alone represented more than one hundred and five years of down-and-dirty experience in the real-world trenches of the restaurant business. Bruce Attebery designed bar and kitchen layouts and knew how to equip same. Ron Stephenson dealt with some one hundred landlords and the problems associated with those locations. Haig Cartozian knew marketing potential and costs. Tom Lee knew personnel and morale management. Bobbi Loughrin was more than capable of analyzing the financial reports. And then there was me. Why wouldn't Charlie tap this fountain of information? It wouldn't have cost a dime and could've saved millions.

I didn't hear of any action to correct the cause of customer count and stock value drops, which would have been the logical things to do in order for Charlie to stay consistent with his reputation as a "company turn-around specialist." In very short order, this beautiful company with its manicured campus was shopped around Wall Street. Madness!

Do I sound bitter? Not really. Sad maybe, because so few can do so much harm to so many. Am I harsh? No—these men can take my opinions.

A successful man is one who can lay a firm foundation with the bricks that others throw at him.—Sidney Greenberg

Marriott Corporation purchased Saga primarily for the volume-feeding portion of the company and proceeded to sell off the other parts including the Black Angus chain. Just as well. In my opinion, Marriott never could manage anything that their daddy didn't start. The Black Angus is back to the basic menu under the management of American Restaurant Group, but more on them in the Epilogue.

Here's some beef for Helen and principals Anwar Soliman and Ralph Roberts, at a recent Henderson, Nevada, opening. I've come full circle—back to where I began—serving.

CHAPTER 20

IS THERE LIFE AFTER
BLACK ANGUS?

I'd know that sound anywhere! We were at six thousand feet, crawling over the ice and snow, sneaking up on what had to be a bull elk breaking branches as he moved. We were in the Manashtash area of the Cascade mountains in Eastern Washington in late fall. My fellow hunter, Dick Dameyer, and I had almost frozen our bippies off in sleeping bags the night before, but now it was all going to be worthwhile. We took our mittens off so we could handle the freezing-cold triggers of our rifles. We stopped again to listen, but what we now heard didn't make much sense. It was a hissing sound, much like a mountain lion, only it was steady. We hunkered down even lower and moved ahead slower when all of a sudden a shadow loomed in front of us. What was going on here? It was way too large to be an animal. And then we saw that it was a damn pickup truck sitting alongside an elk trail.

How in the hell did it ever get way up here? This was the early fifties and it was the first time I had ever seen anything like this. I realized it was a four-wheel-drive rig, but still that had to be some job of driving because it had this apparition filling the whole bed of the pickup. This *thing* in back was what I now know to be a slide-on camper and the hissing sound was created by a small propane heater.

Silence is golden in the wilderness, but we sure broke it with our greetings. They came out of their *cave* dressed as if they were home, and here we were in our parkas and colder than a well digger's butt in January. The only things that gave them away as fellow hunters were the fact they all carried binoculars and the rifles you could see racked in the window of the pickup. What was said wasn't important. It was all I could do to keep from staring inside the little camper, checking out every convenience and comfort. Oh, how I wanted to go inside that lovely warm space and spend the day—to hell with the elk! But I couldn't do that—I wasn't even invited—so I decided to look into this dream machine as soon as I got back to civilization. Next year's expedition would be taken on in comfort!

I put a pencil to my dream and came up short. I was working such long hours that, when I did get some time, I'd better not go hunting with the guys but instead spend it with my wife and daughters. I didn't exactly win awards as a husband and father as it was, but, to be honest, the biggest reason I didn't buy the camper was because I didn't have the money. The fact I couldn't find one made it a little less painful. It was the early fifties and there really wasn't such a thing as a recreational-vehicle lifestyle—you rarely saw them on the road.

During the next ten years I never forgot that dream. Even if I found a camper I liked, it wouldn't make much sense to buy it. I had screwed up my first marriage—I was hardly ever home. Either I was in the office, working the restaurant floor, tending bar, or just enjoying the bar. Not only didn't I have the time to appreciate a camper, now I had no one to share it with. I started thinking about everything involved with owning a camper—even a small one. It would be expensive to buy, plus there would be sales tax, license, and insurance. It would cost money to stay at the mobile-home parks, which were the only places available for RVs in those days. It wouldn't get good mileage like a car so the fuel would cost twice as much and, at thirty-five to forty cents a gallon, that would mount up. I didn't have a garage, so where would I store it? It would be harder to drive and park in the big cities because of its size. It just didn't make any sense!

Well, forget all of the above. I, along with my second wife, Edie, bought a camper in 1962. I had my good friend, business associate, and interior decorator, Bill Teeter, devise a very modern interior for this small space. He even put a fake phone in for atmosphere which was indicative of his humor. (This was long before cellular telephones were ever heard of.) We hired a driver one late afternoon and decided to have a little party in the camper. As we were driving down Denny Way in Seattle, we stopped at a red light and Bill leaned down, reached out the window of the camper with the phone, and hollered at the guy parked next to us, "Hey, it's for you." The guy took the phone with this shocked look on his face just as our driver took off. Our phone was gone forever.

I progressed from that camper to two smaller RVs, then large RVs, then big, beautiful converted forty-foot buses—and so it goes!

When you pull into some of the parks, you can't go outside—people such as the two on the next page are right on top of you. I've stayed with these folks no matter how far or how fast I've traveled. There they are—you don't know how they got there, they just appear. You have to accept it as part of the RV lifestyle. We can't stay inside all evening, so outside we go and the conversation starts again. "How many miles a gallon do you get in that big rig?" "What's the horsepower in there?" "Where you from and where you going?" The first two I'd answer, but I'd lie to that last question. When we converted our first bus in 1981, not many were privately owned, and everywhere we went, the people wanted to know what entertainer was inside or what rock group we were with. It's not my nature to be a snob, but when they asked to look inside, I usually drew the line. When we travel, all we want to do is enjoy the beauty of the different neighborhoods we get to spend the night in and to watch the sun set in a new environment.

As the restaurant chain expanded into the small towns in Washington, Oregon, and California, it became necessary to visit the locations frequently. I found travel by air impossible, and by car a drag, so it made good business sense to purchase a nice new

Some people's image of RV parks. You can tell these people don't belong in the neighborhood—lovely Linda and Colonel Jeremiah greeting us.

A trip in our first bus in 1982 with, from left to right, Me, Gratzi and Bob Anderson (without tiny little curls), Helen, and Sally Johnson Newbery in foreground sans handkerchief uniform.

bus and have it converted. Recalling all the above, do you buy that? Well, let me tell you how it works. I could park in the restaurant lot, usually close enough so we could plug in and have electricity. We'd have dinner at the restaurant, along with a martini or two without having to worry about driving. My third (and last) wife loved it and I got to have my own bed, jammies, and my favorite pillow. A home away from home, and most important, all these advantages were a business write-off, so you've got to go for it. Right?

However, something was happening. Helen and I were falling in love with the motorhome lifestyle. After we left the business, we lost our parking, plug-ins, and write-offs. It didn't make any difference, we were captured by the highways and the byways. We've met fabulous new friends we travel and rally with, and have a nice way to visit old friends and our families without being intrusive.

Our kids and grandkids think we're gypsies. I have this deep need in me to roam and be free to explore and discover, and luckily my wife does, too. If you have ever considered this lifestyle, rent a vehicle and try it. Like certain diets, it's not for everyone. Be careful, though, because you could get hooked. It's a way to experience the wonders of nature, with an ever-changing vista, while sleeping in your own bed. You'll live and move in this neighborhood with America as your backyard—not just to look at but to hike in the mountains, fish in the ocean or some beautiful lake, or walk in the woods and pastures. Now go back to the fork in the road and turn the other way; there's another new world awaiting and something else to see.

Are we RV drivers loved by all the traffic out there? Probably not. I've got a restaurant logo on my bus (Oh, puh-leeze, Anderson), so I get a few waves while moving down the road. I like to think those are always friendly, but sometimes they could be flipping me the rude sign. We do take up a bit of room. Consider this: The Recreational Vehicle Association estimates that nine million of these vehicles are going up and down our highways. In 1994, 441,000 RVs were shipped to dealers. This trend is going to continue, despite all the negatives I mentioned earlier.

The Back-Seat Drivers' Instructors Club left to right: Lou Stewart, Carol Nurcombe, Barbara Patch, Lu Nichols, Julie Sklar, Helen Anderson and Susan Mickeleit

The brain trust. Phil Hamlin and Lisle Hawkins with wives Ruth Hawkins and Millie Hamlin

A rally at the ranch over Labor Day. These coaches are furnished like the most glamorous New York penthouses. Gentlemen, start your engines!

Helen, her son Mike, Christopher, David, me, flanked by grandsons Will and Logan Gee

If I read like a mass of contradictions regarding the RV lifestyle, I know I'm doing it because I have mixed emotions. What I say isn't going to make one wit of a difference to this industry, but I hate to see our highways get too crowded, and that's purely selfish.

Remember, if you don't know where you're going, any road will take you there.

See all these good-looking people in the pictures? I didn't know one of them (except my sister and her husband) before I got my RV. They didn't work for me or know anything about me— thank goodness for small favors. The first photo is the TNT (Tennis 'n' Travel) group and nobody has more fun with the possible exception of the second bunch I call the GNG (Golf 'n' Go) bus group. The TNT group is a little bit younger and a little bit healthier. The GNG group is a little bit older and maybe a little wealthier considering their sport and chariots. I don't know which group will kill me first, but Helen and I love them both. Life is GOOOOOOD!

Sister Suzanne, Norm House, Helen, Norm Sears, waiter, Marilyn House, brother-in-law John Peterson, and Micheline Sears—all members of the TNT group

Me, Terry and Sally Ballard, Helen, Susan Mickeleit, and Barbara Patch— all members of the GNG group

EPILOGUE

LIKE SAND
THROUGH THE HOURGLASS

Time is a river, and as it moves along, you lose some friends and gain new ones. Samuel Johnson said, "If a man does not make new acquaintances as he advances through life, he will soon find himself left alone. A man, sir, should keep his friendship in constant repair." That's all well and good, but friends, like the river, move on and seem to disappear. It's hard to keep them in repair when time and events take you in so many different directions. There are the employees, the customers, the suppliers, and even the bankers who all did a great deal to enrich my life, and I thank them for that. There are the people we worked with on the ranch and those with cattle and drafthorses with whom we dealt. I send salutations to all the people we enjoyed from Eastern Washington. I have compassion for people and I'm happy to the degree that I have that.

If I've zinged a few folks along the way, it's because I'm reminded of those who didn't pay heed to this saying: "Be nice to people on your way up because you're likely to meet them on the way down." It's doubtless good fun to get back at old foes.

I think about people I've known over the years who meant so much to me. Where have all the flowers gone? More like where have all those who have impacted my life— one way or another—gone?

THE RESTAURANT'S
EXECUTIVE COMMITTEE

The man with the bare feet and voice like Sinatra: Bruce Attebery runs his restaurant, Daman's Tavern, located between Bellevue and Redmond, Washington, and plays some golf when Bev let's him.

The young guy selling me coffee: Ron Stephenson, after a long stint with Restaurants Unlimited of Seattle, is on the board and part owner of—are you ready for this?—a company that rebuilds locomotives in Montana. He recently married a lovely lady. Best wishes Ron and Naomi.

The man who saved my ass in the bar one night: Tom Lee plays a fair amount of golf when he's not traveling with his wife, Christine, to visit their son, daughter, and grandkids.

The fellow who shared his table with a stranger: Haig Cartozian has stayed in the marketing world with his consulting company called Market Share Resources and operates out of Ellensburg, Washington. He and his wife, Jan, are also trying to perfect the game of golf.

The lady who advanced women's rights without trying to: Bobbi Loughrin is an executive with the elegant Sorrento Hotel in Seattle, doing well, and can be reached on-line, whatever that means.

That completes the executive committee and I had better stop there or it'll take another whole book. There are many others out there who were instrumental in the chain's history, such as John and Jack who built the buildings for us to play in and the editor who reported on everyone. They know who they are and I love them all. I thoroughly enjoy my life now, but the years building and operating the restaurants were the best years of my life.

Tommie Lee, Millie Hodge (founder and editor of *Stu Who's News*),
Bruce Attebery, me, Bob Robbins (BA director of personnel) and Bob
Anderson, at a recent gathering

THE SAGA OF SAGA

- Ernie Arbuckle and his wife both lost their lives in an unfortunate automobile accident.

- Charlie Lynch is on his third company since Saga's demise and is currently CEO of the Fresh Choice Restaurant chain.

- Founder Bill Scandling wrote an excellent book on his company which is titled *Saga*. He has recently remarried after the death of his first wife.

- Hunk Anderson works with his extensive art collection and enjoys his homes in California with wife Moo.

- Bill Laughlin and wife Jane are still in the Woodside, California, area. Bill is working toward keeping the long-gone Saga alive.

- Jim Morrell and wife Maralyn enjoy their family and home in the Bay area. Jim is a director on several boards and plays a little golf.

- Ralph Pica works with his sons in the building trade in Southern California.

- Fedele Baccio is operating a successful catering company in the San Francisco area, along with Ernie Collins from the legal end of Saga.

- Larry Mindel hasn't called me, so I don't know what's happening in his life.

- The Stuart Anderson Black Angus Cattle Company Restaurant chain is back to serving that great beef (another plug). It's in competent and compassionate hands. The American Restaurant Group consists of people who know the beef and restaurant business. I'm pleased that my name is associated with this group which is owned and operated by Anwar Soliman and Ralph Roberts.

That God in His infinite wisdom and mercy would only let friends and lovers stay close, but that's not the way it works.

Somebody STOP me! I'm getting a little heavy here, so I think I'll go have a martini and a good steak.

Stuart has left the building.

SECTION V

RECIPES

ROASTING

MOM'S ROAST BEEF

This one comes from a ranch east of the mountains and our good friend, Marge Mellergaard.

Serves 8

1 T. oil
2 1/2 lb. eye-of-the-round beef roast
1 medium onion, chopped
1 C. brewed coffee
1 cup water, divided
1 beef bouillon cube
2 tsp. dried basil
1 tsp. dried rosemary
1 garlic clove, minced
1 tsp. salt
1/2 tsp. pepper
1/2 cup all-purpose flour

Heat oil in a Dutch oven; brown roast on all sides. Add onion and cook until transparent. Add coffee, 1/2 cup water, bouillon, basil, rosemary, garlic, salt, and pepper. Cover and simmer for 2 1/2 hours or until meat is tender. Combine flour and remaining water until smooth; stir into pan juices. Cook and stir until thickened and bubbly. Remove roast and slice. Pass the gravy.

• • • • • • • • • • • • • •

HORSERADISH MUSTARD SAUCE

This will keep for weeks in the refrigerator. Try it on your leftover roast.

1 T. mustard seeds
1/3 cup dry mustard
3 T. vinegar, white wine or cider
3 T. sugar
1 T. olive oil
4 or 5 drops of lemon juice
1 T. horseradish sauce

Soak the mustard seeds in hot water for about an hour, drain, and place in a food processor. Add the rest of the ingredients and process, stopping to scrape sides, for about two minutes. Refrigerate. Best if made ahead so flavors blend.

MANOR (OR CASTLE) ROAST
FROM SWEDEN
Called "HERRGARDSSTEK" and dates from the 1800s

Lena Mann, who also enjoys our island, says this is a hearty roast for Sunday dinners on wintry days. It's served with lots of strongly seasoned gravy and is familiar to, and enjoyed by, most Swedes.

Serves 6

3 lbs. rump steak
2 T. butter
1 1/2 to 2 tsp. salt
1 bay leaf
8 black peppercorns
2 carrots
2 onions
3 Swedish anchovy fillets (Don't substitute—try
   Scandinavian specialty stores)
1 T. white vinegar
2 tsp. light syrup (such as Karo or Golden)
1 1/3 cup bouillon

Gravy:
1 3/4 cup strained pan juices
3 T. all-purpose flour
Water
1/2 cup heavy cream
Brandy/gravy coloring/soy sauce, optional

Trim away any membrane and truss up the meat. Brown the butter in a heavy skillet and then brown the roast on all sides. Season with salt and pepper. Add bay leaf, peppercorns, peeled and sliced carrots and onions, anchovies, vinegar, syrup, and bouillon. Cover and let roast simmer for about 2 hours or put in the oven at 325 degrees and baste periodically. As the liquid evaporates, keep adding bouillon or water. Remove roast from the pan and wrap in foil. Let stand for at least 15 minutes before carving in slices.

To prepare the gravy, strain the pan juice and return to skillet. Make a paste by adding a little water to the flour. Stir this and the cream into the pan juice. Cook for about 5 minutes, stirring until smooth and thickened. Season with brandy, gravy coloring, and/or soy sauce according to preference. Traditionally this roast is served with white potatoes, lingonberry preserves and a fresh cucumber salad. This roast is even tastier if prepared the day before.

BAKED STEAK WITH MUSTARD SAUCE

This recipe comes from our good traveling buddies, the Gislasans. Throw some new red potatoes in the pan, dribble a little butter on them, season, and let them cook alongside the meat.

Serves 4

2 1/2" thick sirloin steak, 2 lbs.
Salt and freshly ground pepper to taste
1 medium onion, finely chopped
1 cup catsup
3 T. butter, melted
1 T. lemon juice
1 small green pepper, sliced
Fresh chopped parsley, 1 small bunch
Worcestershire sauce, a few drops

Preheat broiler. Place steak 4 inches below broiler. Sear both sides. Remove from oven and drain off fat. Season with salt and pepper. Mix all ingredients and pour over steak in pan. Place in 425-degree oven for 30 minutes. Remove from oven and transfer to a platter. Pour mustard sauce over, sprinkle parsley on top and serve.

Mustard Sauce:
2 T. butter
2 T. barbecue sauce (any commercial brand)
2 T. Worcestershire sauce
2 T. dry mustard
2 T. cream

Mix all ingredients with melted butter, except cream. Heat over medium burner until bubbly. Add cream and heat just until hot but don't boil. Serve over baked steak.

• • • • • • • • • • • • • •

ROAST TENDERLOIN OF BEEF
WITH MADEIRA SAUCE

Serves 8

1 whole beef tenderloin, 4 1/2 to 6 pounds
1 tsp. salt
1/2 tsp. coarse-ground pepper
1/2 tsp. dry mustard
2 T. chutney, minced
4 T. soft butter
1 cup thinly sliced, fresh mushrooms
1/2 cup canned condensed beef consommé, undiluted
3 T. Madeira wine

Place the tenderloin on a rack in a shallow roasting pan. Mix together the salt, pepper, mustard, chutney, and 2 tablespoons of the butter. Rub the top of the tenderloin with this mixture. Preheat the oven to 450 degrees and leave it there. This is one cut of beef that needs to be cooked fast and hot. Insert the thermometer in the meat. Roast for 25 to 40 minutes or until the thermometer registers 140 degrees for rare or 160 degrees for medium. The meat is best served rare. When it's reached the proper temperature, remove it to a hot platter and keep warm until ready to serve. Add the sliced mushrooms and consommé to the drippings in the roasting pan. Stir over high heat, scraping the bottom of the pan to loosen all the flavorful bits. Boil these meat juices for a minute and then add the Madeira and the remaining 2 tablespoons of butter. Simmer just until butter is melted, stir, and pour into a warm sauceboat to offer with the roast.

• • • • • • • • • • • • • • •

BLUE CHEESE STUFFED
FLANK STEAK
WITH WILD MUSHROOM SAUCE

6 servings

Meat Seasoning:
- 2 T. extra-virgin olive oil
- 2 T. dry red wine (Merlot or Cabernet Sauvignon)
- 2 cloves garlic, minced
- 1 T. chopped fresh Italian parsley
- 1 T. chopped fresh rosemary
- 1 T. chopped fresh thyme
- 1/2 tsp. medium-grind black pepper
- Salt to taste

Stuffing:
- 1 box of frozen (or one bunch fresh cooked) chopped spinach, thawed and well drained
- 1 egg
- 1/4 cup dried bread crumbs
- 3 ounces Oregon bleu cheese, crumbled
- 1 T. extra-virgin olive oil
- 1 T. pine nuts, roasted
- 1/4 cup porcini mushrooms, rehydrated in warm water for 45 minutes, drained and finely chopped
- 1 clove garlic, minced
- Salt and pepper to taste

1 flank steak (1 1/2 to 1 3/4 lbs.) butterflied
1 T. extra-virgin olive oil
1 T. butter

Wild Mushroom Sauce:
2 T. chopped shallots
1/2 cup dry red wine (Merlot or Cabernet Sauvignon)
1/4 cup beef stock
1/4 cup chopped portobellow or chanterelle mushrooms

Preheat oven to 350 degrees F.

In a small bowl mix olive oil, wine, garlic, parsley, rosemary, thyme and pepper. Mix thoroughly, then salt to taste.

After butterflying (this is slicing almost all the way through the entire piece of meat sideways, so you have twice the surface of the original steak), open steak on work surface and thoroughly rub both sides with above meat seasoning.

In large bowl, mix spinach, egg, bread crumbs, cheese, olive oil, pine nuts, mushrooms, and garlic, then salt and pepper to taste. Spread spinach mixture evenly over the steak. Starting at one end, roll the steak up jelly-roll style. Tie it with white, cotton string at two-inch intervals.

Heat a large skillet to medium-high, add olive oil and butter, then quickly brown the steak on all sides. Remove it to an oven-proof dish and bake for 55 minutes for medium-rare, or longer if you prefer it more well-done.

Using the pan in which the steak was browned, quickly sauté the shallots for the Wild Mushroom Sauce until transparent. Deglaze the pan with the red wine. Add the beef stock and mushrooms. Reduce heat to medium and simmer for 10 minutes or until reduced and slightly thickened.

When steak is cooked, thinly slice steak on the diagonal and lay flat on serving plate. Top with Wild Mushroom Sauce. Serve with a wild-greens salad.

• • • • • • • • • • • • •

PAN- OR STIR-FRYING

STEAK STIR-FRY
WITH KIWI TERIYAKI

Serves 4

1 lb. sirloin tip steak or bottom round, cut in thin strips across grain
2 kiwifruit
1/4 cup white wine
l/4 cup soy sauce (we use 1/2 low sodium)
2 T. brown sugar
l to 2 cloves garlic, minced
1 tsp. freshly-grated ginger root
2 T. olive oil, divided
12 mushrooms, sliced
12 Chinese pea pods
l 1/2 cup bean sprouts
2 tsp. cornstarch

Mix the kiwi, wine, soy sauce, brown sugar, garlic cloves, and ginger in a blender or food processor and place in zip-lock bag or shallow bowl with the beef. Marinate at least one hour. Pour 1 tablespoon olive oil in wok or heavy skillet and sauté the mushrooms, pea pods, and bean sprouts. Pour these into a bowl and keep warm. Add 1 tablespoon olive oil and half of beef to pan and sauté briefly until done. Pour into bowl with vegetables and sauté balance of beef, reserving marinade. Pour vegetables and balance of beef back into pan. Add cornstarch to reserved marinade and add to mixture stirring constantly until thickened.

Serve over rice or fresh Asian noodles.

RICE: Let's talk about rice. Health- and taste-wise there is no comparison to whole grain, long-cooking rice. The California rice co-ops put out a select brown rice that can't be beaten in my estimation. It has a wonderful nutty texture. It comes in either a plain brown paper bag or the standard, plastic, see-through bag and has ten times the character of quick-cooking white rice. It does take about a half hour longer to cook but well worth it. Or experiment with some of the different types on the market, such as Texmati, Balsamatic, black sticky, and the like.

TIP: Keep fresh ginger in the freezer in a zip-lock baggy and grate frozen as needed. Use slightly more this way as it is quite airy when grated frozen. Much better than dried ginger out of a spice can.

SPICY BEEF IN CRISP ARUGULA NEST

Serves 4

Put a pot of your favorite rice on to cook.

> 1 T. cornstarch
> 1 T. soy sauce
> 1 T. oyster sauce
> 1 tsp. sherry
> 1 lb. arugula leaves, washed and dried (use spinach or mustard greens if you prefer). Cut into 1/4" strips. Be sure they are thoroughly dried as splashing of grease could occur when cooking.
> 1 lb. tri-tip steak or other tender boneless beef, trimmed of all fat
> 2 T. cornstarch
> Seasoned or freshly ground pepper to taste
> 1/2 cup sweet onion or green onions, chopped, including some of the tops
> 2 cloves garlic, crushed
> 3/4 cup peanuts
> 1/4 cup vegetable or olive oil

Combine cornstarch, soy sauce, oyster sauce, and sherry and set aside.

Slice beef into 1/4" strips (slightly freeze for an hour or so to make it easier to slice). Then slice again across grain so you end up with small pieces about the size of a raisin. Pour 2 tablespoons cornstarch over the meat and sprinkle with pepper to taste. Stir well to mix and set aside.

Coarsely crush peanuts (put in plastic bag and crush slightly with rolling pin). Put them in a glass dish and microwave for 3 minutes or until toasted. Set aside.

When the rice is done, heat the wok or heavy skillet over high heat. Add 1/4 cup vegetable oil to pan or enough to make it at least an inch deep. When hot add arugula greens, a small handful at a time (watch out for grease splashing), stirring constantly for about 10 seconds until they turn a little translucent, and remove with a slotted spoon onto thick paper towels. Continue to do this until all the greens are cooked. Keep warm in oven.

In the same pan, add or take away oil as necessary to leave about 1 tablespoon, and stir-fry 1/4 of the beef at a time just until brown, transferring each batch to a bowl until it's all cooked.

Next, add onions and stir-fry for 2 minutes, add garlic and stir-fry another minute. Pour beef back into the pan and add the soy mixture.

Stir until it thickens and the meat is hot. Serve immediately over the greens. Sprinkle the toasted peanuts on top.

If you like a spicier taste, use a few drops of chili oil in the vegetable oil when you're frying the meat or add crushed red peppers to the beef. The leftovers would be great in a salad.

Serve with a fresh beet salad.

· · · · · · · · · · · · · ·

GRILLING

NEW YORK STEAK
WITH PANCETTA LATTICE
AND SUN-DRIED TOMATO BUTTER

This recipe and the one for Blue Cheese Stuffed Flank steak were contributed by Lynn Kastner who has a degree in Culinary Arts. She had the good fortune to be related to Sally Johnson Newbery whom you met in Chapter 4. Thank you, Lynn. They're delicious!

6 servings

Sun-Dried Tomato Butter:
> 3/4 cup (1 1/2 sticks) butter
> 1 T. Dijon mustard
> 7 whole sun-dried tomatoes packed in olive oil, drained and minced
> 1 large clove garlic, minced
> 1/4 cup Italian parsley, minced
> 1/4 cup freshly grated Parmesan cheese

Steaks:
> 6 New York steaks, 12 to 14 ounces each, about 1-inch thick
> 1/3 lb. thinly sliced pancetta (If you can't buy pancetta, which
>   is Italian bacon, use side pork thinly sliced.)
> 1 T. dry mustard
> 1 T. coarsely ground black pepper
> 1 tsp. salt

Process the butter and mustard in a food processor until smooth. Add the sun-dried tomatoes, garlic, parsley, and Parmesan cheese. Pulse the machine on and off until the ingredients are just incorporated. Lay a large piece of plastic wrap out on a flat surface. Shape the butter into a one-inch thick log down the center of the wrap. Roll the plastic around the butter to enclose it completely and store in the refrigerator until ready to use. (Can be prepared up to one week in advance.)

To make the pancetta lattice on the steaks, cut 3 deep diagonal slashes lengthwise and 2 slashes crosswise on the top of each steak with a sharp knife. Take care <u>not</u> to cut all the way through to the other side of the steaks. Ideally, when you buy the pancetta, ask the butcher or deli to slice it thin for you. Insert the strips into the slashes to form a lattice. This can also be done ahead of time.

Prepare the grill for cooking. Mix the dry mustard, pepper, and salt, and rub this mixture over both sides of the steaks.

Grill the steaks 3 to 4 inches above the hot coals, starting with the bacon side up and turning once, 10 to 12 minutes for medium-rare meat. As the steaks come off the grill, top each one with 1 or 2 of the one-inch thick slices of the sun-dried tomato butter. Serve at once. Offer the extra butter slices on the side.

You might like to serve this with cooked orzo (rice-shaped pasta) tossed with fresh parsley and Parmesan.

• • • • • • • • • • • • • •

Marinated Flank Steak

Serves 6

1 1/2 lb. flank steak
3/4 cup oil
1/4 cup soy sauce
1/4 cup honey
2 T. vinegar
3 T. onion, finely chopped
1 large clove garlic, minced
1/2 tsp. ground ginger, or 1 tsp. freshly ground

Score flank steak on both sides in a diamond pattern and place meat in a shallow pan or a large plastic baggy. Combine the rest of the ingredients and pour over the steak. Marinate in the refrigerator all day, or overnight, turning occasionally. Broil 5 to 7 minutes per side, depending on how you want it cooked. Slice very thin across the grain to serve.

• • • • • • • • • • • • • •

CARTOZIAN BEEF SHISH KABOBS
WITH VEGETABLES

The following recipe for Shish Kabobs was submitted by Haig Cartozian who was my VP of Marketing (you met him in Chapter 8). As you can probably tell from his last name, there's a large amount of Armenian involved here.

Serves 6 to 8

4 lbs. choice grade beef (top sirloin), cut into approximately
  1 1/2" cubes
1/2 cup olive oil
1/2 cup dry white wine
Juice of 1 lemon
1 medium onion, chopped fine
2 T. oregano
1 T. cumin
1 T. allspice
Fresh, ground pepper
3 cloves of garlic (crushed or chopped)
3-4 bay leaves, broken in pieces
Vegetables (small onions, green pepper, red pepper,
  mushrooms, cherry tomatoes)

To make marinade, combine oil, wine, lemon juice, onion, oregano, cumin, allspice, pepper, garlic, and bay leaves. Stir well, add beef chunks, and marinate 12 to 24 hours in a large zip-lock baggy. Periodically work the meat around inside the marinade. Or use a sealable plastic storage container and shake periodically. Refrigerate while marinating.

Prior to cooking beef, wash vegetables, core, and cut to desired size for placement on skewer. Set aside.

Lift beef out of marinade and thread onto metal skewers. Begin with a slice of pepper, then beef, and alternate vegetables–for color and cooking flavor. Continue until skewer is almost full or to serving size. (Some prefer to cook the beef separately from the vegetables.) Cook over a hot grill or glowing charcoal, turning and basting frequently with the marinade. Cook to taste (approximately 10 to 15 minutes for medium rare.) Place on platter with or without skewers. Garnish with pasley and lemon wedges. Serve hot.

• • • • • • • • • • • • •

STEAK WITH BRANDIED ONIONS

        1 lb. lean sirloin steak
        Salt and pepper to taste
        4 T. butter
        1/2 tsp. garlic powder
        4 medium onions, sliced
        1T. parsley, chopped
        Dash of brandy

In a heavy skillet, melt the butter and garlic. Add the onions and cook over medium heat, stirring frequently, until they turn a caramel color. Add parsley and brandy and let simmer another minute or two. Season the steak with salt and pepper and grill 4 to 7 minutes per side, for rare to well, whichever is your preference. Transfer steak to a platter, spoon the onions over the top and serve.

• • • • • • • • • • • • • •

BRAISING

HELEN'S SPAGHETTI SAUCE

Serves 8

2 - 3 T. olive oil
1 lb. beef stew meat with all fat removed and cut in bite-size pieces
1 lb. hamburger, the leaner the better
1 cup sliced mushrooms
1 cup chopped celery
1 medium onion, chopped
4 cloves garlic
1 whole carrot
1 large can chopped tomatoes
1 small can tomato paste plus one can water
1 small can tomato sauce plus one can water
1/2 tsp. Italian seasoning (rub between fingers as you add to bring
    out flavor)
1/4 tsp. dried oregano (or 2 tsp. fresh)
1/4 tsp. dried basil (or 2 tsp. fresh)
1/4 tsp. dried rosemary (or 1 tsp. fresh)
2 large bay leaves
10 whole dried red peppers
Parmesan cheese
1 16-ounce package spaghetti, linguine, angel hair, or other pasta

Brown stew meat in oil. Add hamburger and cook until browned. Drain off all fat. Add vegetables and cook, stirring frequently, until softened. Add all liquids and spices. Continue to cook, partially covered, and stir for at least 2 hours (more is better). Add water if it gets too thick. **Remove bay leaves, carrot, and red peppers before serving. This is very important as the red peppers are very hot.** Pour some of the sauce into the cooked spaghetti to keep it from sticking together. Put spaghetti on the plate, add sauce and top with Parmesan cheese.

It's always better the next day. The sauce freezes well.

Serve with any fresh green vegetable you've blanched or with sautéed spinach, chard, kale, or other greens.

NEAT TRICK: If you have to hold your pasta and keep it warm, instead of completely draining after cooking, just pour off half the water and add cold water. This will stop the cooking process and keep it warm and moist until needed.

● ● ● ● ● ● ● ● ● ● ● ● ● ●

BEEF STROGANOV

This is the classic version of this delicious Russian dish.

Serves 4 to 6

1 T. dry mustard
1 T. sugar, divided use
2 tsp. salt
4 to 5 T. olive oil
4 cups of onion, thinly sliced and separated into rings
1 lb. fresh mushrooms, thinly sliced
2 lbs. fillet of beef, trimmed of fat (sirloin can also be used)
1 tsp. freshly ground black pepper
1 pint sour cream

Combine the mustard, 1 1/2 teaspoons of the sugar, a pinch of the salt and enough hot water (about 1 tablespoon) to form a thick paste. Let this mixture stand at room temperature for about 15 minutes.

Heat 2 tablespoons oil in a heavy skillet over high heat until a light haze forms above it. Drop in the onions and mushrooms, cover the pan, and reduce the heat to low. Stirring from time to time, simmer 20 to 30 minutes or until the vegetables are soft. Drain them in a sieve, discard the liquid, and return the mixture to the skillet.

With a large, sharp knife, cut the fillet across the grain into 1/4-inch wide strips. Heat 1 to 2 tablespoons oil in another heavy skillet (I use my wok) over high heat until very hot but not smoking. Drop in half the meat and, tossing the strips constantly with a large spoon, fry for 2 minutes or so until the meat is lightly browned. With a slotted spoon, transfer the meat to the vegetables in the other skillet and fry the remaining meat similarly, adding additional oil, if necessary. When all the meat has been combined with the vegetables, stir in the remaining salt, the pepper, and the mustard paste. Stir in the sour cream, a tablespoon at a time, then add the remaining 1 1/2 tsp. of sugar and reduce the heat to low. Cover the pan and simmer 2 or 3 minutes until the sauce is heated through. Taste for seasoning.

To serve, transfer the contents of the pan to a heated platter and serve with rice, wide egg noodles, or very thin French fries.

• • • • • • • • • • • • • •

GROUND BEEF

MEAT SARMA

Armenian-style wrapped grape leaves and beef

**Serves 8 for appetizers,
6 for main course**

16 oz. preserved vine leaves (available in deli-section at groceries)
2 lbs. lean ground beef
1 large sweet onion, chopped
Salt and pepper
1/4 tsp. cumin, or to taste
1 tsp. oregano
1/2 tsp. allspice

1 medium-size lemon
1 large (or 2 small) cans of chicken broth
1 cup long grain rice
3 large cloves garlic
1/4 cup olive oil
1 medium bunch of parsley (chopped fine)

Rinse grape leaves in cold water. Keep moist for best handling.

Sauté rice and half of onion in oil for about 20 minutes. Remove from heat and add half of the spices. In a separate bowl, mix the ground

297

beef and other half of onion and work mixture by hand until well blended. Add sautéed rice and knead until slightly sticky. Add parsley and balance of spices and knead again until well mixed.

To shape sarmas, place vine leaf, shiny side down, on a work surface. Snip off stem, place about a tablespoon of meat mixture near stem end, fold stem end and sides over stuffing, and roll up firmly.

Line base of heavy, skillet-type pan with vine leaves (use damaged ones); then, as the sarmas are rolled, pack them close together in layers. Sprinkle each layer with lemon juice. (You may also use a light sprinkle of garlic powder or crushed cloves if this suits your taste.) When rolls are completed, cover with any remaining grape leaves. Add the chicken broth with any remaining lemon (juice or thinly sliced lemon). Lay a heavy, oven-proof plate on the sarmas to create a slight pressure on them so they keep their shape while cooking. **Cover** and place over medium heat until it just starts to bubble. Reduce heat to simmer and gently cook for 1 1/2 hours. Drain cooked rolls and arrange on a hot serving dish. Garnish with parsley and lemon slices.

Sarmas are served hot as a main entree but can also be used as an appetizer. You can eat them cold anytime.

• • • • • • • • • • • • • •

FRANKS IN SILVER

Cyndy threw this recipe in for good measure. It's great!

Serves 8

>2 cups minced all-beef frankfurters
>1/4 cup grated cheese
>1 1/2 tsp. prepared mustard
>2 hard-boiled eggs, chopped
>1 tsp. Worcestershire sauce
>2 T. sweet pickle relish
>1/4 tsp. chili powder
>2 T. mayonnaise
>Frankfurter rolls

Combine all ingredients. Fill frankfurter rolls. Wrap securely in foil. Place on barbecue for 15 to 20 minutes. Turn often. Serve hot.

Serve with some oven-baked fries.

SALADS

CRUNCHY ORIENTAL BEEF SALAD

Serves 6 to 8.

1-1/2 lb. flank steak (or leftover beef roast) sliced across the
    grain (with knife slightly angled) into thin strips
1/2 cup water
2 T. *each* dry sherry, rice wine vinegar and vegetable oil
1 T. *each* soy sauce and oyster sauce
2 tsp. sugar
1 tsp. *each* garlic powder and beef bouillon granules
Flavor packet from a 3 oz. package of instant oriental noodles,
    beef flavor
1 to 2 T. olive oil
1 or 2 heads of your favorite lettuce, torn into bite-size pieces.
1 cup *each* shredded red cabbage and thinly sliced celery
1/2 cup slivered almonds
4 green onions (including tops) sliced
Noodles from oriental noodle package, broken into 1/2" pieces
2 T. toasted sesame seeds
Ginger dressing (recipe follows)

Ginger Dressing:
1/2 cup vegetable oil
6 T. sugar
4 T. rice wine vinegar
1 tsp. salt
1/2 tsp. *each* ground ginger and black pepper.

Combine the water, sherry, vinegar, oil, soy sauce, oyster sauce, sugar, garlic powder, bouillon granules, and beef flavor packet from the noodle package. Pour over the beef, cover, and refrigerate 1 to 2 hours or overnight to marinate. It's always nice to get the hardest part over with the night before.

Combine all of the ginger dressing ingredients and whisk to blend. Refrigerate.

The next day, stir-fry the beef in a little olive or vegetable oil until tender. Drain and refrigerate beef at least 45 minutes. When you're ready to serve, take out a large salad bowl and combine the lettuce, cabbage, celery, almonds, green onions, and the broken noodles.

Serve with a homemade chunky applesauce and crunchy French rolls.

ERICA SALAD

Serves 4 to 6

You may wonder what this one has to do with beef. Well, let me tell you. We stopped at a beautiful Black Angus cattle ranch at the foot of the Sierras in Gardnerville, Nevada, where we were greeted by Jim and June Rolph. It turned out to be one of those instant friendships. We caught fresh trout out of their pond and ended up staying for a wonderful dinner and fun evening. Jim did a lot to keep the Black Angus breed pure. We didn't get to keep Jim on this earth as long as we would have liked, but have stayed in touch with June. She served this salad that night.

6 T. vegetable or olive oil
3 T. vinegar
Salt and pepper to taste
1 sweet onion, chopped
1 pkg. frozen or 1 can drained, French style green beans
4 hard boiled eggs, chopped
3 T. mayonnaise
1 tsp. prepared mustard
2 tsp. vinegar
1/2 tsp. salt
4 strips bacon
1 head lettuce, new leaf, butter, or other curly-leafed type

Combine oil, vinegar, salt, pepper, onion and green beans in a bowl. Combine eggs, mayonnaise, mustard, vinegar and salt in another bowl. Fry bacon until crisp. Crumble into small bits.

To assemble, put beans on a bed of lettuce, put egg mixture on top, and finish with a sprinkling of bacon crumbs. Delicious.

This salad goes well with a grilled rib-eye steak and sautéed mushroom caps.

• • • • • • • • • • • • •

MISCELLANEOUS

ORIGINAL RANCH BREAD

Serves 8

1 loaf French bread or combined French and sourdough
1 cup bread crumbs
1 cup Parmesan cheese
2 T. garlic powder
2 T. paprika
1/2 cup (1 cube) butter

Mix crumbs, cheese, garlic powder, and paprika thoroughly. Melt butter. Dip each slice of bread into the butter, then into the topping. Bake at 450 degrees four to five minutes. I prefer a toaster oven. And now you know!

• • • • • • • • • • • • •

GARLIC/CHEESE BREAD

1 loaf French bread
Paprika

Garlic/cheese spread as follows:
1/4 cup (1/2 cube) butter or margarine
2 large cloves garlic
1 1/2 tsp. lemon juice
4 oz. each jack & cheddar cheese, shredded
2 T. grated Parmesan cheese
1 T. mayonnaise
1 T. minced parsley
1/4 tsp. oregano, crushed dried leaves

Make garlic spread by combining butter, lemon juice, and garlic and mix well. Combine mixture with mayonnaise, parsley, and oregano and blend. Add cheeses and mix again. Split loaf in half horizontally. Spread each half with the cheese/garlic mixture. Sprinkle with paprika. Bake at 350 degrees for 5 minutes and then place about 6" under the broiler for another 3 to 5 minutes until it's golden brown (watch carefully so it doesn't burn). Cut and serve in napkin-lined basket.

• • • • • • • • • • • • •

STUART & SARAH'S BEAN MIX

For all of you who have had one of the great meals in the big party barn at the ranch, you will remember the wonderful baked beans. Well, now you can do them. Of course, sitting in that pot over an open fire, where we used special woods for flavor, might have had something to do with the flavor.

Serves 20

1/2 lb. thick-sliced bacon, diced
3 medium onions, diced
1 1/2 cup ketchup
2 1/2 tsp. BBQ spice (a dry spice available at grocery stores)
3/4 cup brown sugar
3 cans (28 ounce each) B&M baked beans, drained

Sauté the bacon until half cooked. Add onions and sauté until trans-lucent. Add remaining ingredients and simmer uncovered for 1/2 hour. Drain the beans and add to mixture. Simmer for a least 1/2 hour.

Note: This bean mix can be made and frozen <u>before the beans are added</u>. You can then use it as needed for smaller quantities.

• • • • • • • • • • • • • •

BLACK ANGUS
POTATOES AU GRATIN

This was a much-requested recipe in the early days when this was the only other choice besides a baked potato at a Black Angus Restaurant

Serves 4 to 6

1 1/2 lb. potatoes
Salt
2 T. (1/4 stick) butter
1 T. finely chopped onion
1 garlic clove, minced
2 T. flour
1 1/2 cup hot milk
1/2 cup shredded sharp cheddar cheese
1 tsp. freshly grated Parmesan cheese
Salt & freshly ground pepper or seasoned pepper
1/2 cup shredded cheddar
2 T. grated Parmesan
1/2 tsp. paprika for topping

Boil unpeeled potatoes in lightly salted water until tender. Cool, then peel and cut into 1/4" slices. Layer slices in buttered casserole.

Preheat oven to 350 degrees. Melt butter in medium saucepan, Sauté onion and garlic until translucent and stir in flour until mixture is smooth. Gradually add hot milk, stirring constantly. Stir in 1/2 cup cheddar cheese, 1 teaspoon Parmesan cheese, and continue cooking until cheese is melted. Season to taste with salt and pepper. Pour over potatoes in casserole, sprinkle with cheeses and paprika, and bake for 25 to 35 minutes, or until golden brown.

• • • • • • • • • • • • •

GRAVY OR BROWN SAUCE

1 to 2 T. cornstarch
Small amount of water or milk to dissolve cornstarch
Pan drippings
Milk and/or potato water
Salt & pepper to taste
1/2 tsp. Kitchen Bouquet
Red wine (optional, see below)

Mix 1 to 2 T. cornstarch with a small amount of water and set aside. Set pan (remember to use a pot-holder) with drippings on burner on medium. Using wire whisk (spiral type works best), and stirring constantly, add milk, approximately 1/2 cup per serving (we use non-fat and even a little water from the potatoes we boiled). When it starts to boil, add the cornstarch gradually, whisking continuously, until it is the desired thickness (if it's too thick, add a little more milk or water). Salt and pepper to taste. Then stir in about 1/2 tsp. Kitchen Bouquet. It'll get rave revues.

Of course, Chef Ray says it's not a brown sauce without wine. This can easily be done by first adding a little wine (I like Burgundy) to loosen all that good meat and drippings that are stuck to the pan. It's called deglazing. Then proceed as usual.

Pour over potatoes and sprinkle with additional cheddar, Parmesan and paprika. Bake 20 minutes. Place under broiler just until brown and bubbly. Serve immediately.

HUMMUS

Serves 10 as appetizer

1 15-ounce. can garbanzo beans (chickpeas)
1 1/2 tsp. cumin
6 T. tahini (sesame butter)
1/2 cup lemon juice
3 T. olive oil
3 crushed cloves of garlic
Paprika
Sea salt
Fresh parsley for garnish
Crackers or vegetables for dipping

Drain garbanzo beans and save liquid. Add beans to blender with all other ingredients except parsley. Add enough of the garbanzo bean liquid to make a smooth paste. Refrigerate. Spread on rice or corn cakes if you're watching calories.